BILKO: BEHIND THE LINES WITH PHIL SILVERS

BILKO: BEHIND THE LINES WITH PHIL SILVERS

Mickey Freeman
and
Sholom Rubinstein

*Dedicated to my wife Anne Freeman for
all the wonderful years of laughter, living
and loving together.*
M.F. New York

*Dedicated to my love, Bess Adele, my wife
and best friend for six decades, and to
our children, Jill Slavin, Henria King and
Michael Rubinstein.*
S.R. Atlanta

First published in Great Britain in 2000 by
Virgin Publishing Ltd
Thames Wharf Studios
Rainville Road
London W6 9HA

A catalogue record for this book is available from the British
Library.

ISBN 1 85227 807 2

Phototypeset by Intype London Ltd
Printed and bound in Great Britain by C.P.D. Wales.

Contents

Acknowledgements

Our thanks to Mohan Pai for his splendid help in finding us a publisher and for his generosity in allowing us to use his resources and talents in the making of this book. His assistance has been invaluable. We have only met Mohan on the Internet, but we hope we will soon be able to meet him face to face.

We gleaned numerous facts about Nat Hiken from the fine article David Everitt wrote for *TV Quarterly* (1990, Volume 3).

The following helped us with advice, reminiscences and material:

Paul Uber, Ron Simon, Coleman Jacoby, Gabby Jacoby, Allan Melvin, Nick Saunders, Jean-Pierre L. Trebot, Steve Everitt and Mick Clews of the Phil Silvers Appreciation Society.

Our editor Anna Cherrett for excellent suggestions and revisions. She is also expert with the commas.

Claude Cain III – a man who has two doctorates and deserves another for his knowledge and appreciation of the Phil Silvers Show. He has been unstinting of his time and his tape collection.

Preface

I spent four years in the army during World War II and four years writing and producing *McHale's Navy*, but I never saw military manoeuvres like I did on *Sergeant Bilko*. I'm referring to the platoon's mad dash to get a good position in front of the camera and close to Phil Silvers. Being a good actor was important, but not as important as being nimble and shifty. For the men of the platoon, it was called survival of the fastest.

The *Bilko Show* was one of the classic examples of 'gang' comedy and, as a producer, I learned a lot from it about dialogue distribution – how to keep a crowd of talented, and agile, actors happy with their parts and to discourage them from counting lines and close head shots. Of course, carrying a machete always seemed to help.

Phil Silvers doesn't need any words of praise from me. He was brilliant. Bilko was a part he was born for. But I really have to admire his platoon. They sparkled in the glow of Phil's talent and his magic spread to them to make the show the success that it was.

Si Rose, Los Angeles, California, 1999
(Mr Rose was a writer for Bob Hope and Edgar Bergen. He was the producer of *McHale's Navy* and writer/story editor of *Dukes of Hazzard*.)

It's forty-five years since we filmed the *Bilko Show*. The laughter has never stopped, the recognition has never stopped, and the applause has never stopped. The only thing that has stopped are the residuals.

Two words often change the course of a person's life: 'Not Guilty', 'I do', and 'You're fired'. My two-word mantra was: 'But Sarge . . .!'

Mickey Freeman, New York City, 1999

1 The Travel Diary of Pvt Zimmerman

Lindy's Restaurant on Broadway and 52nd Street, the late 1950s: the temple for those who practised the religion of show business, where communion was taken not with wafers and wine, but with cheesecake and coffee. Here came the notables from the special worlds of nightclubs, the New York stage, radio, the borsht belt and the fast-growing television industry. To worship and be worshipped. To take their bows for the smash shows and their lumps for the bombs.

Luminaries such as Milton Berle, Red Buttons, Jerry Lester, Irving Mansfield and Goodman Ace gathered to try out the latest quips and be the first to purvey the freshest stories hot off the Hollywood telephone lines. The illustrious traded insults with each other and with the inscrutable waiters. And, more often than not, the waiters won.

Five storeys above Lindy's was a rehearsal hall called Nola Studios – the womb of many hit television shows of the era. It was a place where concepts were polished, lines rehearsed, scenes blocked, camera moves planned and punch lines honed. The better you did upstairs, the better table you got downstairs. I'm sitting on a hard folding chair studying my Zimmerman lines when Nat Hiken, our resident genius, the creator, producer and director of the still-to-be-aired *Sgt Bilko Show* comes by and I say: 'Nat I gotta tell you. This script is funny – not radio funny, not television funny – but funny, funny.' Nat's lips moved, not a smile but a kind of twitch: 'Thanks Zimmerman. You know something – I'm going to make you famous.' I look down on my script. My best line is: 'But Sarge . . .' As an actor with a contract I figure that from 'But Sarge' I might make a living. But famous???

But the decades that have elapsed since then have proved that Nat Hiken, the quiet, gentle, wise man, was right. I'm not famous, but Zimmerman is. Over the years I've taken bows for him all over the world. The Bilko Show is like the British Empire – the sun never sets on it. At any given moment, the machinations of Ernie Bilko and his platoon are causing severe laughter somewhere.

Trinidad, 1964. The late Abel Green, editor of the show biz Bible *Variety*, is walking along the street with his wife, my wife Anne, and myself. Abel says: 'Mickey, they're calling Zimmer-mahn.' 'Nah,' I say modestly, hanging my head and scuffing my shoe, 'that's how they talk to the tourists. They call everyone "mahn".' Abel calls over one of the locals: 'What did you call this fellow?' 'Mahn – that's Zimmermahn – from television.'

Hong Kong, 1979. The manager of the local Hilton recognises Zimmerman and throws a shindig in his honour.

Chicago, 1980. George Jessel, vaudevillian and one of the foremost fundraisers and after-dinner speakers, has just gone to the big dais in the sky. I'm filling some of his commitments. I check into the Palmer House where I'm scheduled to speak that evening. The bellboy takes me to my room and performs the classic bellhop choreography – he opens the curtains, hangs the bag, turns on the air-conditioning and flips on the TV. He looks at the screen and loses his professional cool. 'Hey mister,' he yells. 'You're on television.' As coincidence would have it, Bilko was on in the afternoon in the Windy City.

It's 1984 and I'm working as a stand-up comic on a series of cruises that take me from Palermo to Athens to London to Leningrad. The ship makes port in Guernsey, one of the Channel Islands.

My wife Anne and I are in a charming tea room called 'La Chouette' noshing the local delicacy – scones spread with blackcurrant jam and cream and sipping strong English tea. The owner of the place has been staring at me since we came in and she finally comes over and says: 'Aren't you Zimmerman from the telly?' 'Guilty,' I confess, 'How did you know?' 'We get Sgt Bilko over here every week but only in black and white.' I say: 'That's the way we made it.' She clamps her hand over her mouth: 'You really are Zimmerman. I'll be blowed.'

Fade out and fade in to 1985, New York. Sgt Bilko and gang are on local TV every night at 11 p.m. and once again Zimmerman is out on the streets of the Big Apple taking bows. The magic of television – Zimmerman is always 29. I get older, the fans get heavier, their hair gets thinner and they're wearing designer bifocals. But the new breed of Zimmerman's fans is college kids and youngsters whose parents and grandparents were the original viewers. And for the watchers, young or old, the platoon on the screen never ages. But if you tried to recreate Company B of the Fort Baxter Motor Pool today, not answering the roll call would be Pvt Doberman, Pvt Paperelli, Cpl Barbella, Pvt Mullen, Pvt Gomez, Pvt Fender, Sgts Grover, Ritzik, Pendelton, Col Hall and Sgt Bilko. Also not responding would be Billy Friedberg, Arnie Rosen and Nat Hiken. For a non-combatant unit, a very high mortality rate.

It's very chic to dump on American television, but

when a show that was filmed in the late 1950s still generates new, enthusiastic fans over forty years later, it must be recognised as a classic. The *Bilko Show* does not trade on nostalgia. The gags, the situations and the characterisations hold their own in today's world. The *Bilko Show* proves that wit, intelligence and taste can create a product that is literally timeless. It is electronic history, part of the culture of America and many other nations.

People such as Nat Hiken, Neil Simon, Joe Stein, Tony Webster, Coleman Jacoby, Arnie Rosen, Barry Blitzer and, of course, head writer Billy Friedberg created the words and characters that Phil Silvers and company brought so brilliantly to life. As I watch the re-runs, I think to myself how valiant those make-believe soldiers in the platoon were as they fought to make CBS safe for the three 'Rs': Ratings, Re-runs and Residuals.

2 The Start of Something Big

Generals through the ages, from Genghis Kahn to Colin Powell, have exploited the platoon for military purposes, but it took a short, middle-aged, non-belligerent civilian to turn the platoon into a source of laughter and entertainment.

The platoon system did not reach its ultimate glory until Nat Hiken created the aggregation of eccentrics who made up Company B of the motor pool at Fort Baxter, Roseville, Kansas. These reluctant warriors fought the good fight against truculent carburettors and hostile drive shafts under the sharp eye and flexible ethics of Sergeant Ernie Bilko, a.k.a. Phil Silvers. Bilko was a first in television – the con man as father confessor.

Hiken's platoon was not only victorious in the television wars but led the way for future TV shows, from *McHale's Navy* to *Hill Street Blues*. The formula is simple: a group of characters engaged in the same line of work are placed in the same locale each week – the barracks of *Bilko*, the garage of *Taxi*, the squad room of *Barney Miller*, the PT boat of *McHale's Navy*, the precinct house of *Hill Street Blues*, the emergency room of *ER*. Each week these people exercise their established foibles, fight the brass and perhaps achieve a small victory – only to slide back into their predetermined niche just in time for the closing commercial, ready to let it all hang out in the next episode.

The platoon was a new experience for me. Up to that point I had been a stand-up comic working alone at single engagements. Suddenly I was a man with a contract, the same place to go every day, the same group of actors to work with, the same payday each week. If it had not been for the make-up, I would have sworn that I was in the civil service.

For the four, fun-filled, satisfying years during which we shot 144 episodes of the *Bilko Show*, it was my feeling that all of us were individually and collectively happy. And why not? Unlike the real army we had no hikes, no policing of the parade grounds, and no KP.[1] In our unit the front was always the place to be – because the front meant being closer to the camera.

Any professional involved in any aspect of comedy will testify to the many details that must be perfectly in sync to make a laugh work. When you're out there alone it's hard enough but when the gag depends on the rhythms of ensemble playing there's no room for mistakes.

The man who made everything work was Nat Hiken, creator, writer, producer, director – genius. Hiken's greatness lay in understanding people and how they behave. Nat cast dramatic actors in comedy roles. Bea Pons, who played Sgt Ritzik's wife, once told me that she never realised that she could get laughs: 'When I opened a window and proclaimed: "Hello world, my husband is a nut", I opened a window on a new career.'

Maurice Gosfield, who played Doberman, once asked for time off to audition for *Actor's Studio*. Hiken said:

---

[1] Kitchen Police – American army slang for kitchen duty, including fun things like mopping floors and scrubbing pots.

'Doberman, if you improve your acting and diction in any way – you're off the show.'

As actors, we knew little about the creative anguish endured by the writers for each week's episode. Come Monday at Nola's Rehearsal Studios, we'd sit around a table with head writer Billy Friedberg who would read us the opus that he considered magnum – for that week anyhow. As Billy read he would vigorously pump his right leg up and down, a common enough nervous habit that many people have. Billy had developed it into an art form, a kind of sit-down dance routine that pre-dated break dancing by at least two decades. He rarely had anything to be nervous about – he always got laughs in the right places – and at the end of his reading, this hardened group of comics and comedy actors would break into genuine applause.

But a good script is only part of the making of a television show. The technical problems of getting a half-hour show on film (videotape had not yet been put into use) was a formidable operation. A show had to be rehearsed and filmed in five days. Then came the complications of editing the film by splicing together master shots, inserting close-ups and exteriors, and re-recording audience reactions (without laugh machines) into the right places. A tremendous amount of skill and know-how was involved. In spite of the fact that Hiken had spent many years in television – the *Martha Raye Show*, the *Fred Allen Show* and other comedy vehicles – he was a stranger to film and its techniques. Fortunately, CBS had assigned a man by the name of Al De Caprio to be camera director.

Up to that time most filmed TV shows were shot just as movies were. Just before the *Bilko Show* was to go into production, CBS, New York became aware of new techniques that were being used on the West Coast.

I Love Lucy – CBS's hottest property – was being filmed with three interlocked film cameras. One camera took the master shot and the other two captured the other angles that the action dictated.

The three-camera technique was a big time saver, but it created a host of new problems – how to light the set, how to mike the actors, and how to edit the three strands of finished film. In the three-camera set-up the TV show is treated as if it were a stage production. The show is shot in exact sequence. However, instead of plush theatre seats, the audience sits in hard bleachers, and microphones are hung overhead to record laughter and applause.

As Al De Caprio tells it, one day he was summoned to the office of a CBS VP who told him that CBS, New York, wanted to film the *Bilko Show* in three-camera style similar to *I Love Lucy*.

'Go out to Desilu in California,' said the VP. 'It's a very busy and crowded set. Each camera has a cameraman and a dolly pusher. There are assistant directors, floormen, prop people, grips, still photographers. Go out and mingle with the crowd. Just wear this badge. No one will notice you.'

'I felt more like an employee of the CIA than CBS,' said Al. He arrived on the *I Love Lucy* set with his wife Carmen and did his best to blend in.

To the eye of the layman a TV studio in full blast looks like Herald Square at high noon. But a producer who signs the payroll cheques knows exactly how many people should be on his floor at a given moment, and Al's cover was blown in less than two minutes when a voice boomed over the loudspeaker: 'You – what are you doing down there?' Al flashed his badge and timidly said: 'I'm with CBS.'

Thoughts of firing squads and cyanide pills flashed

through his mind. Before he could make a break for freedom an excited and angry Desi Arnez was down on the floor yelling: 'Who are you, what are you doing here?' Al had an inspiration. 'This is very embarrassing,' he said. 'I'm here with my wife Carmen. By the way she speaks Spanish.' The presence of a Spanish-speaking lady brought out the gallant Latin in Desi. Carmen and Desi exploded in a burst of Spanish dialogue and all of a sudden the New York invader was invited to be an honoured observer.

Some time later, Desi called and invited Al to come to work for Desilu, but he was too deeply involved with the *Bilko* production to be able to leave. In later years, after Hiken had left, the platoon hoped that Al would be given a chance at directing the show but the brass felt that he was more valuable in the technical area. It was not until the show went off the air that he went on to direct numerous comedy and variety shows.

Flashback – Tuesday of any shooting week! Most TV shows start rehearsing bright and early. Anyone coming in a minute after 9 a.m. is in trouble. At the *Bilko Show* the call was for 11 a.m. This gave Phil Silvers the chance to check the morning line and the scores for the previous day's baseball, hockey, football, basketball, stickball, and hop scotch. If it moved, Phil bet on it. When we picked up our scripts on Tuesdays, the previous day's 45-page diamond-in-the-rough had been polished down to a 30-page sparkling gem.

So help me, the pages we threw away then would be a hit series today.

One o'clock and Silvers and Hiken need their daily fix – 'Lunch at Lindy's' administered by their favourite waiter, a man named Yager who delivered the yoks with the lox.[2] I have often felt that 'Lunch at Lindy's' was what kept the show on the East Coast. Forget the palm trees and the Californian climate. Forget the glamour and bikini-clad starlets. When it came to cheesecake there was no contest. A real cheesecake mayven[3] – and Phil was certainly an expert – understood that even young starlets grew old but Lindy's cheesecake was baked fresh every day.

By Wednesday we were all expected to know our lines. Not a big trick for a professional performer. For most of us there were not a great number of speeches to learn. But, week after week, Silvers amazed us. He had most of the lines and he always lived up to the basic creed of the actor 'Know Thy Words'. We would look at him with amazement and appreciation. Phil would glare back and say: 'Sure, I know my lines but I live like a monk.' Not exactly like a monk! How many monks have a private line to their bookmaker?

On Thursday we moved to the Dumont Studios on 67th Street where we turned into instant soldiers. The sets looked legitimate, the props were genuine, and the uniforms and fatigues were government issue. For the next two days, for all practical purposes, we were GIs. The barracks looked so real that you would often find an actor taking a nap in one of the bunks.

On Thursdays we'd find Karl Lucas – who played Kadowski – zonked out in his bunk. Karl was a big energetic man and we couldn't understand why he was always so tired. One day, after a rewarding day of

[2] For those who are Broadway-slang challenged, 'Yok' is show biz for belly laugh, and 'lox' is a kind of smoked salmon. Translation of this phrase is therefore 'served the jokes with the smoked salmon'!
[3] 'Cheesecake' was the Hollywood slang for these luscious young women, while a 'mayven' is a Yiddish term for a person with special knowledge – an expert.

shooting, I said to Karl: 'This will move you to a new station as an actor.' Karl replied: 'Right now the only station I worry about is on the Brooklyn subway where I have the night shift in the change booth.' We realised that Karl was moonlighting and that he didn't have enough confidence in the future of the *Bilko Show* to leave his job with the city.

Friday was magic time! Show time! The call was for 9 a.m. Final camera blocking. Dress rehearsal at 1 p.m. The day the first show was to be filmed, when we got dressed we discovered that a conscientious wardrobe mistress had sent out all the fatigues to be cleaned and pressed.

Out on the set it looked like graduation day at West Point and Hiken screamed as if he were a drill sergeant and we were real soldiers. He barked in a voice we had never heard: 'Everyone on the floor! Find dirt and roll in it! Step on each other!' And not until we were properly squalid did he let the cameras roll. From then on the wardrobe mistress was careful to keep the fatigues impeccably filthy at all times.

After dress rehearsal, Hiken would make his last-minute changes and the audience of 300 was ushered in. Since the show was not yet on the air and a big secret as far as the public was concerned, there were no ticket requests. A fugitive from a Damon Runyon story – Red Cullers – cajoled and coerced senior citizens, innocent bystanders and out-of-towners into our bleachers. There was only one requirement for admission – you had to be ambulatory.

But in the trade, word had got around that the *Bilko Show* was the place to be on Friday afternoons. Stars such as Cary Grant, Myrna Loy and Jack Benny could be found on the hard bleacher benches, screaming with laughter. One of our regulars was Milton Berle, who would leave his own rehearsal to roar at our antics. After one of the filmings, Uncle Milty announced to Phil and the cast: 'This is the funniest show I've ever seen.'

It all seemed marvellous, except for one little thing – our shows were not on the air. We'd been coming to the studio for twenty weeks, performing for 300 appreciative spectators without a single episode being on the air. CBS kept saying: 'Put it in the can. We'll find a slot for you one of these days.' We'd leave the studio with the sound of laughter and applause in our ears and come home to the dubious stares and suspicious questions of wives and friends. Phil Silvers summed up the way we felt during those weeks of waiting. In his book he tells of going to visit his mother and she asked: 'Phil, are you still doing television?' Phil nodded and his mama said: 'Here's twenty dollars. You should have eating money while you're doing television.'

Phil Silvers, as the star of the show, would do the warm-up each Friday. This was a chore he detested. As Bilko he could hide behind the character he was playing, but going out as Phil Silvers left him too exposed. Several times he would be in the bathroom throwing up just before he was due out on the set.

The warm-up always ended with Phil introducing 'the real star of our show – Duane Doberman'. Maurice Gosfield, as great a slob in real life as the character he portrayed on screen, would waddle out and cock his head to one side and say in his nasal whine: 'Hello.' Pandemonium! The audience would scream with glee. Doberman was a great visual laugh. Just looking at him was enough.

The show was performed in sequence, the cameras only stopping to reload film. Any other director would have asked to retake sequences that did not play as planned. Not Nat Hiken. If De Caprio would suggest a retake so that a shot might be framed better, Nat would say: 'They came, they saw, they laughed. Leave it alone.' Consequently, the careful student of early Bilko episodes will notice glitches here and there that could be found on live shows but never on filmed ones. After the twentieth or so show Hiken's frustrations began to show. He did a little first-class ranting: 'How do I know if the home audience will like a show about a bald-headed sergeant with horn rimmed glasses?' He went to Hubell Robinson, the programming VP of CBS, and extracted a promise that a day and time would be set the following week.

One day we came to rehearsal and a very serious Hiken announced: 'We've got our time slot.' The platoon cheered as if it were VE day. Nat went on: 'The *Sergeant Bilko Show* is scheduled for Tuesday night at 8.30. Right in the middle of the *Milton Berle Show*.' This time slot was known in the industry as Death Valley. We looked at each other. Our fate was sealed. Opposite Mr Television we would become the Unknown Soldiers.

D-Day arrived, Tuesday 8.30 p.m. The first Sgt Bilko programme was broadcast over the CBS network. On Wednesday we returned to the studio and congratulated each other. We were euphoric. Our success was assured.

Then came the ratings. We found out that D-Day stood for Disaster Day. It seemed as if no one was watching. But like optimistic baseball fans, the cry became 'wait till next week'.

Next week came. Even before the official ratings, the actor's personal Arbitron[4] told us that things were not getting better. The day after a show a TV performer senses reactions. The doorman says: 'Funny show last night, Mr Freeman.' A taxi driver will call out, 'Saw you

[4] The TV and radio rating system that evaluated the popularity of shows.

on TV last night,' and even your local neighbourhood butcher will take his hand off the scale long enough to give you the thumbs-up sign.

The third week I was too nervous to watch the show at home for fear that my wife would be tuned into Milton Berle.

In today's high-powered, impatient television world the kind of ratings we got would mean immediate cancellation, and the un-aired shows would remain in the can – despite the fact that they cost $65,000 each, in 1957 dollars.

But Hubell Robinson was a man of conviction who trusted his own taste and he refused to let the low ratings stampede him. He arranged for Phil Silvers and the platoon to appear on the *Ed Sullivan Show*.

On Sunday night we were all on stage and Bilko put us through a mock military drill and, judging by the studio audience, it was a hilarious segment.

The following Tuesday the ratings began to move upward and the very next Tuesday we topped the *Milton Berle Show*, the first time in seven years that the Texaco Theatre was not in the number one spot.

A few weeks later an army recruiting officer called Phil to tell him that the *Bilko Show* had done more to increase military enlistments than all of their public relations efforts. Of course, those new enlistees must have been very upset when they discovered that the real army was not the laugh-filled life that they saw on the TV tube.

But, for me, this was the beginning of four years of fun and games.

3 The Doberman Mystique

Whatever it took to be the nation's number one slob –
Duane Doberman had it. Pvt Duane Doberman of
Company B of the Motor Pool never found out that neat-
ness counted. He was a loser, a slovenly fat man who
shuffled rather than walked, a man who mumbled rather
than talked. But the audience adored him.

The actor who created the character of Duane
Doberman was Maurice Gosfield. Gosfield was able to
play the part without make-up because, when it came
to personal habits and manners, the real Gosfield and
the fictional Doberman were one. The word fastidious
was not part of either his vocabulary or his life. Nat
Hiken used to say: 'An actor works all his life in the hope
that he will leave a mark on the world. Maurice Gosfield
will leave a stain.'

When Hiken hired him, Gosfield had been around for
a number of years as a journeyman character actor
whose ambitions were limited to the next job. But the
adulation of the television public moves in strange and
mysterious ways and Pvt Duane Doberman became as
well known as Sgt Bilko.

With some people, success goes to the head – with
Maury it went to the stomach. It was a world of second
portions and the right wines to go with them. We all
knew that Gosfield was a diabetic but we could tell by his

feeding habits that he took absolutely no care of himself. He guzzled carbohydrates, devoured bread and drenched his food in rich sauces. Sugar-laden desserts were not a course, but a career.

After the character of Doberman took the public's fancy, Gosfield was a star. Like most stars he was surrounded every night by beautiful women. They were attracted by the popularity of Duane and they figured that the man who played such a lovable shlump was just acting. But by morning they were gone – they quickly discovered that Gosfield was really Doberman in rumpled civilian clothes. Maury may have had all the trappings of a star, but he was really a very lonely man. He lived by himself on Madison Avenue and 48th Street and his family lived in Philadelphia. They had little to do with each other.

Al Melvin and his wife, the late Harvey Lembeck and his wife, and Anne and I were very close and we often had dinner together. We made a point of inviting Maury to our homes. After the third dinner at our house, when once again the walls were splashed with food, the upholstery was freshly stained and there were new cigarette burns on the end table, Anne announced: 'I'm sorry to say this, but he is banned from the apartment. From now on when we invite Maury, we have a new activity – eating out.' Carol Lembeck protested: 'How can you be so mean, he's really very sweet.'

Sometime later, the Lembecks had us all, Gosfield included, over to dinner. She served spaghetti and sauce, and was pleased to see Maurice carefully tuck his napkin under his chin, continental style. Dinner was delicious and the laughs were as plentiful as the food. When we got up from the table, Gosfield removed the napkin to reveal a shirt and tie, not to mention Carol's hand-embroidered tablecloth doused in marinara sauce. Another household was lost to Gosfield.

One day at lunch, during the early days of the series, we were startled when Gosfield announced that he had just done a commercial for a weight loss product. Hoots and jeers from the platoon: 'Who are you – before or after?' 'I'm both,' he explained. As 'before' he was seen on screen wearing his regular clothes, which always looked as if they were about to explode. As 'after' he came on wearing a suit, in the same material, that was at least two sizes too big – thus creating the illusion that he had lost many pounds. Of course, this spot was for a local television station and long before the days of the 'truth in advertising' law.

During the filming of the series, Silvers still kept up a heavy personal appearance schedule in places such as Las Vegas, Miami and Chicago. Gosfield became a feature at those gigs because local producers would always remind Phil: 'Don't forget. Bring Doberman along.' Much to Silvers' credit, he displayed no ego and always took the 'real star' along. Gosfield's contributions to those evenings was 'Hello' and a couple of 'But Sarges'.

The public perception of Doberman as a funny funnyman was so ingrained that even these few words got big laughs and tremendous applause. In restaurants, people would send champagne to Maury's table, deliver gifts for him to the studio and extend invitations to openings, galas and all the 'in' parties.

One of Broadway's most respected and successful press agents was Eddie Jaffe, and Hiken and Silvers used his apartment when they were working on scripts. The apartment was also frequented by many show biz characters whose antics inspired some of the scenes that were used in the Bilko episodes.

One day, some of us in the platoon received invitations

to Eddie Jaffe's birthday party that was to be held aboard a Hudson River Day Liner moored at 42nd Street. As befitted a press agent of Jaffe's stature, the ship and the food had been promoted for free by his cronies.

My wife, Maury and I went together and when we arrived we were amazed at the number of people on board. It appeared as if everyone in the Manhattan telephone book had been invited. The party fare was magnificent and opulent – a very long table was covered with every conceivable kind of antipasto, meat, salad, and dessert known to voracious man. There was no finger food.

As we watched the guests, a pattern of behaviour emerged. A guest would take a plate and expectantly take his place in line. But there were no serving pieces, and not a sign of cutlery anywhere. There were no waiters around to ask for help and after five or ten minutes of anticipation the guest would return his plate to the pile and leave.

We observed lines of hankering guests lining up and we saw lines of voracious invitees leaving the boat – all with the same frustrated expression on their faces. When it came to food, Gosfield was not a man to accept defeat. He stood, plate in hand, squarely in front of the table. His eyes were welling up with anticipation and starving suspense. I borrowed a familiar line from one of the Bilko scripts: 'Let's go, Doberman, I can't stand to see a fat man cry.' But Gosfield was transfixed, mumbling: 'Wait, wait.'

Anne and I lost patience and started to leave. Just then one of the 'hosts' appeared and announced: 'We're down to sixty. Break out the cutlery and the serving pieces.' As if by magic, knives, forks, napkins and the much-needed serving pieces appeared and the party was on.

What a *tour de force* of organisation. To invite the immediate world and feed only the immediate family.

Watching Gosfield in action was awe-inspiring. The man didn't eat – he inhaled his food. It was a smorgasbord orgasm.

One of the fringe benefits of being in a hit TV show is your entrance to the glorious world of the 'freebie'. It started with our sponsor who would send each and every one of us two cartons of Camels a week. R. J. Reynolds wanted to make sure that every time we lit up in public the world would see that we smoked Camels.

As the ratings soared, the gifts began to be more impressive. Nat Hiken had a home in Montauk, which is on the tip of Long Island. Gosfield spent most weekends out on Fire Island.

As a result of a publicity stunt, Nat and Maury each wound up with a fibreglass motorboat. On the set, Doberman would boast about the boat and about his superior seamanship. He claimed that he had been trained in navigation when he was in the military. My gut feeling was that Gosfield had prepared the navigation charts for Amelia Earhart. One day I was doing a show for the Coast Guard at the Manhattan Beach Station. After the show, one of the commanders came backstage to thank me for coming and, as he was leaving, he said: 'Please tell your friend Doberman to buy a book about boating or take some lessons. We've had to tow him in off Fire Island three times. With his sense of direction it's a wonder that he finds his way to the studio every week.'

I shared the story with Harvey Lembeck and Al Melvin, but we agreed to let Gosfield's myth sail on.

Our laughter at Doberman was always tinged with love because Maury was a sweet, gentle man. We understood that here was a nervous, insecure actor who had become a star through no fault of his own.

When we did scenes that required a lot of physical exertion, Doberman would sweat so profusely that I once muttered to Nat Hiken: 'If Doberman could run like his make-up we could enter him in the Olympics.' In one scene, Silvers was standing in front of the platoon, upwind of Doberman, and he broke us up, as only he could do, when he looked Gosfield straight in the eye and said: 'More Arpege, Doberman. More Arpege.'[1]

After we finished shooting the *Bilko Show* it was not easy for any of us to get parts in other TV shows. We were so identified with the series that casting people could only see us in uniform. For Gosfield it worked the other way because the character of Doberman had become famous throughout the world. Gosfield was booked on quiz shows, talk shows and guest appearances on many variety shows.

At the end of the 50s, television was moving westward and so most of the actors who had played platoon members drifted out to California. The only eastern survivors were Paul Ford, who had played the Colonel, Walter Cartier, the fighter, who played Private Dillingham, and myself.

One day I called Earl Wilson, the columnist, to give him a line for his column, and he told me that Maury Gosfield was in Lenox Hill Hospital. The next day Anne and I went to visit him. When we came into the room he was sitting on his bed dangling his feet. I said: 'Hello, Maury, how are you?' 'Mickey, it's great to see you.' I used my standard opening line for hospital visits: 'What's a nice fella like you doing in a place like this?' He

---

[1] Before designer perfumes, Arpege was one of the most popular fragrances in the US and Europe.

shrugged: 'I have high blood pressure and diabetes but they tell me that they're ready to discharge me.' I was puzzled that he never acknowledged Anne. He knew her as well as he knew me.

Just then dinner was brought in and Gosfield's tray was placed in front of him. We were chatting and all of a sudden I saw that Maury had picked up a fork and put it into his soup. 'What are you doing? You're supposed to eat soup with a spoon.' After a moment of embarrassed silence, he said: 'It's my eyes. The diabetes got to them. But the doctors say it might be only temporary.'

Anne caught on first, and with a tear rolling down her face said: 'Hello Maury.' His eyes followed her voice and he called out: 'Hey – it's Annie. Great to see you.'

As he said 'great to see you' we realised that Gosfield was blind.

Gosfield was about to be discharged from Lenox Hill and the doctors had arranged for him to be sent to the Will Rogers Memorial Hospital in Saranac Lake. This institution is dedicated to the care of show people from all areas of the industry.

Maury kept asking: 'Mickey – what will I do there? It's 400 miles from New York . . . I'll lose all my contacts.' A person in Gosfield's condition needed assurance. 'Maury, you know this business – when they want you they'll find you wherever you are, even in Saranac Lake.'

As it turned out, Will Rogers Memorial was a great move for Doberman. In showbusiness, if you are or were a star, you are always treated like a star. Especially by people in the industry. When Doberman arrived at the hospital he was THE BIG NAME of that moment. And whether he could see it or not, the red carpet was rolled out for him. Paul Ford and I resolved to do as much as we could, via long-distance telephone, to keep the Doberman mystique alive. I would call the operator at the hospital and say: 'This is Private Fielding Zimmerman of Company B of Sgt Bilko's Motor Pool. Col Hall wants to speak to Pvt Duane Doberman.'

She would chuckle and announce over the PA system, so that the whole hospital could hear: 'Pvt Doberman, pick up the nearest phone. Your commanding officer, Col Hall, wants to talk to you.'

Actually, all she had to do was ring his room, but this was a lady who understood the egos of performers. We wanted Maury to feel that the world still cared about Duane Doberman.

Maurice Gosfield never did get back to the Madison Avenue apartment. He died in 1964. The funeral was at the Riverside Memorial Chapel in Manhattan. Paul Ford was on tour with *Never Too Late* so Nick Santly, a very good actor who played on many *Bilko Shows*, and I were the only representatives of the television world.

It was a very simple, short ceremony. I suppose I should have been thinking solemn, serious thoughts, but my mind kept coming back to the weekly warm-up. Silvers would introduce all the members of the platoon and then he would say: 'Here is Private Duane Doberman.'

Before Maurice could open his mouth, a voice on the PA would break in: 'Tell Doberman that his laundry came back.' With his great sense of timing, Silvers would pause and look at the audience and say: 'They wouldn't accept it.'

I said to myself: 'Maurice Gosfield, maybe they wouldn't accept your laundry but 27 million people not only accepted you – they loved you.'

4 The Company Cook and His Tasty Dishes

In the real world, the army mess is a place to feed the troops. In the world of television comedy, the company mess is not for eating – it's a place to cook up plots, dish out laughs, and roast superiors.

During the first twenty or so episodes of the *Bilko Show*, the mess sergeant of Fort Baxter was a character named Sowicki. The part was played by a very fine actor, Harry Clark. Nat Hiken had chosen Harry because he spoke fluent Brooklynese, a dialect that depends as much on a certain shrug of the shoulder or a hand gesture as on the spoken word. Harry portrayed the typical army chef – a skilled artisan who could take perfect ingredients and in no time at all turn them into a culinary nightmare.

Harry Clark had an impressive string of acting credits, including *Wish You Were Here* and *Kiss Me Kate*. At the time we were filming *Bilko*, he was doubling in the Broadway hit *Will Success Spoil Rock Hunter*, which starred Jayne Mansfield and Tony Randall.

Before becoming an actor, Harry had been a physical training teacher and athletic director at Sha-Wan-Ga Lodge in the Catskills. His love of sports never left him and any time he had a free moment, Harry was engaged in some sort of physical activity. Four-wall handball was his particular love and his nemesis.

One day, during our lunch break, Harry rushed away to the 'Y' to play his last game of handball. Television during the day, eight performances of a Broadway show a week, and a violent game of handball any time he had a free half-hour was not the formula for a long life. Harry was the first casualty of the platoon and we felt his loss keenly.

Hiken's requirements for the actor to play the new chef were very specific: a rough-looking, tough-talking comedy performer with the technical skill to come off as a real person. Actors looking for a job will stop at very little, and several would-be mess sergeants claimed to be graduates of both Actors' Studio and Cordon Bleu. Hiken kept explaining that he didn't want a real cook, just a real actor. Four or five 'chefs' passed through the Fort Baxter kitchen, but none of them could come up with the flavour that Hiken wanted.

One day I received a phone call from Kevin Pines, the young casting director of the *Bilko Shows*. 'Do you know where I can reach a comic named Joe E. Ross?' If the casting director of *The Gong Show* had called to ask for the telephone number of Sir Laurence Olivier, I couldn't have been more surprised. Joe E. Ross worked strip clubs, stags, and bust-out joints. And his private life was on the same high plane – as far as I know, he never had a relationship with a woman for which he didn't pay.

Phil Silvers and Nat Hiken had been shopping in Florida at Mickey Hayes' 'Haberdashery' at the Roney Plaza and Joe E. was there negotiating for his annual new undershirt. When he was introduced to the star and creator of *Bilko*, he invited them to a local bistro where he was appearing. Just as a lark, Nat and Phil decided to watch Ross in action. That night, the two of them and six other people constituted the total audience.

It's tough enough to be good when you've got a full

house to work to, but only eight people out front can turn any act into a human sacrifice. Despite the fact that it was a bad night, Nat and Phil saw a quality, which they remembered. And so Kevin Pines was assigned the task of tracking Ross down. I called Charlie Rapp, the Catskill talent booker. The contact for Joe E. Ross was the American Guild of Variety Artists in Florida. Kevin called Florida and was referred to the AGVA office in California and they in turn informed him that his quarry was working at the Blue Hawaii in Honolulu.

Since I was merely an actor, the front office did not keep me informed about day-to-day casting machinations, and I completely forgot about Joe E. Ross.

One day, I walked into rehearsal at the Nola Studios and there was Joe E. in full glory: pointy, patent leather shoes, tuxedo pants and a ruffled formal shirt that he must have cut from his mother's kitchen curtains.

We greeted each other warmly, and when Hiken realised that we knew each other he said to me, tongue in cheek: 'Ask him if he has any daytime clothes.' At the first rehearsal break I said to Joey: 'What kind of rehearsal outfit is this – who do you think you are, Caesar Romero?' Joe E. had a logical answer: 'This is my first time and I didn't know how long the rehearsal would last and I've got a gig tonight.' I don't know what he was worried about – he was only separated from his jacket and tie by two blocks. He was living at the Hotel Bryant on 54th Street.

At lunch, Joey explained the intricacies of being hired for the *Bilko Show*. It was as if Nat Hiken had been writing the script of his life:

JOE E: I almost blew the job.
ME: What do you mean?

25

JOE E: There I am in Hawaii working in this club. The club is owned by a comic – so he works one week and I work the other. The week I was off there was nothing to do except the three Bs.

ME: The three Bs?

JOE E: Beach, Broads and Booze.

ME: Doesn't sound bad to me.

JOE E: Bad? It was great. It was the way I wanted to spend the rest of my life.

ME: So, why didn't you?

JOE E: One night at 1 a.m. I'm in bed screwing this acrobat. Mickey, did you ever screw an acrobat?

ME: No, the gods have not been that good to me. I once spent a night with a fire-eater in Pittsburgh . . .

JOE E: We were in such a complicated position that when the phone rang it took us five minutes to get untangled. I picked up the phone and said: 'What do you want?' A voice says: 'This is Kevin Pines, the casting director of the *Bilko Show* at CBS.' So I hung up and I start trying to figure out how I can get back into the same position with the acrobat. An hour later the acrobat said to me: 'Who was that on the phone?' I explained that it was a smartass pretending that he was from CBS in New York. CBS doesn't call me at 1 a.m. She explained that it was only 10 a.m. in New York. This broad knew what time it was – all over the world.

ME: So?

JOE E: I called the desk and I asked who called me from the lobby and they said that it was an outside call from New York from CBS. So, I called back and I spoke to this guy Kevin Pines and he said: 'Why did you hang up on me?' I never heard of a name like Kevin.

ME: Certainly not at one in the morning?

JOE E: I never heard of it at any time. I said: 'Kevin, what's this all about?' Kevin explained that they wanted me for a guest shot on the *Sergeant Bilko Show* and they would pay my round trip fare and could I be there on Monday. I said OK and I hung up. I turn around and the acrobat is getting dressed. And I say to myself – where am I running, the temperature is 82, the ocean is blue, every day is gorgeous and I never had a woman who could do a back flip in bed.

So, I picked up the phone and sent a cable to Kevin Pines saying: 'Ignore phone call – unable to accept booking.' I hang up and say to her, don't get dressed, and we're back in the sack. A couple of hours later the acrobat and me are eating breakfast in the coffee shop and all of a sudden everyone is congratulating me on my big chance.

ME: How did everyone know?

JOE E: How often do we get a call from CBS in New York? And the switchboard operator was a big mouth. Then the boss came over to congratulate me. And I told him that I had cancelled out. The boss said: 'Joe, how could you do that. A chance like that? What's gonna happen to you here. If you're lucky you'll wind up a beachcomber. We're talking here about the number one television show in the country.' I told the boss that I had already sent CBS a cable saying I'm not coming. The boss said: 'If you call them now, you can intercept the cable.' When I got Kevin on the phone I had to convince him that I was really going to show up and to ignore the cable that he would receive. So here I am.

Despite Joe E.'s unusual perception of real life and its values, in front of the camera he delivered much more than Hiken had ever anticipated. In no time the character he portrayed – Mess Sergeant Rupert Ritzik and his 'oo, oo, oo' – became a household word.

In later years, when the *Bilko Show* finished filming,

Nat Hiken's project was *Car 54*. By that time Hiken thought so highly of Joe E. that he made him one of the stars of the new series. A couple of years later, Joe E. starred opposite Imogene Coca in an ill-fated series called *The Caveman*. The odds are against any performer being involved in leading roles in three major series in a single lifetime. But, Joe E. was not any performer.

On TV all of Ross's shows were family-oriented, but Joe E.'s real life was X-rated. He used to tell of the time he was driving down to Florida and a young lady asked to join him on the trip. He agreed to drive her. She asked to stay with him in Florida, but he refused because he said: 'Mildred, look – I just finished with a marriage and I'm not in the mood to be involved.'

But as the miles rolled by she worked on him and finally he agreed to let her stay in his apartment. 'You can stay but you have to understand the rules. You know I bring broads home any time of the day or night, so when I come in with anyone I'll tell them that you're the maid.'

Two nights after they settled in the apartment in Miami, at three o'clock in the morning, in comes Joe E. with the lady of the minute. As they walked into the apartment and Joe E. flipped on the lights, Mildred jumped out of bed, naked, and grabbed a rag and started to dust the furniture.

Then there is a story that Joe E. told on himself. He had taken one of his several wives on a wedding trip to Florida. A few days later some of his friends, very embarrassed, came to him and said: 'Your bride is turning tricks all over Miami.' Joe E. was incredulous: 'I can't believe it. She promised me not to do it during our honeymoon.'

His approach to women was not the only weird thing about Joe E. Money also brought out strange reactions.

He never really had money until the *Bilko Show*. One day, he came into rehearsal and announced to the platoon that he had bought two thousand shares of stock, at a dollar a share.

This was something that he had never done before and it had caused him a sleepless night. He couldn't understand why he had exchanged good money for a piece of fancy paper headed GREAT WESTERN CHEMICALS. We checked the papers to see how his investment was doing – it wasn't listed.

Joe E. mumbled something about it being an over-the-counter stock. Because he was so nervous about the deal we suggested that he call his broker to unload the stock. He claimed he couldn't do that. We said that every broker was reachable by phone. Not this one. This was a character he had met at Hansen's Drugstore – the famous hangout for actors – while the 'broker' was having a prescription filled. I remarked: 'Now, I know why it's called an over-the-counter stock.' Joe E. asked me to go down to Hansen's with him and negotiate with his 'broker'. Sure enough, the 'broker' was there getting a refill on his prescription. He proved to me that the transaction and the company were both legitimate but, since Joe E. was so uncomfortable with the deal, he gave him his two thousand dollars back, in cash.

Two days later, Joe E. insisted that the entire platoon meet him on the street in front of Lindy's. There stood a twin-finned, second-hand, gold-coloured Cadillac convertible. Joe E. had been walking down Broadway along the block where the used car dealers had their showrooms – it was known locally as 'thieves row'. The Cadillac beckoned and in no time the two thousand dollars had changed hands once again. But, after three months of trying to keep the gold-coloured lemon running, Joe E. sold it. He had it all figured out: 'There are better ways of being screwed than by greedy mechanics.'

Prostitutes were his passion. In a just world, Joe E. should have died during a moment of erotic frenzy in the arms of one of the ladies he so adored. But life is more prone to accident than to justice and Joe E. had to take second best. He breathed his last as he performed for a senior audience of his fellow residents at the California condominium complex in which he lived.

Of all the people in the world, I never expected Joe E. Ross to die not only with his boots on but fully clothed. Even though he did not die in the saddle, it is rumoured that on the day of his death the flags on Eighth Avenue – New York's Boulevard des Hookers – were lowered to half-mast.

I found out recently that history is not complete in the memory of only one man. It has to be confirmed by additional facts uncovered by other researchers.

In September 1999 I received a telephone call from Ray West who told me that he was an optometrist living and working in the UK. He had two hobbies – the Marx Brothers and the Phil Silvers Show. He visited the United States often and pursued his hobbies wherever he went. On a recent expedition he had found Joe E. Ross's grave.

Mr West reported to me that on the headstone the following words were carved: 'I HAD A BALL!'

That was Joe E.

5 Mike Todd's Taylor-Made Acting Debut

The big movie of the spring of 1957 was Mike Todd's production *Around The World in Eighty Days*, based on the novel by Jules Verne. Mike Todd had so much going for him: a tremendous advertising budget, Todd AO (one of the early formats of wide-screen cinematography), dozens of major stars and outstanding sets – the breathtaking splendour of some of the most spectacular vistas in the world. Not to mention a wife who was one of the most beautiful women in the world, Elizabeth Taylor.

Billy Friedberg and Tony Webster, playing off the popularity of the picture, came up with a Bilko script entitled: 'Around the World in Eighty Hours'. The fictional Mike Todd offered a $20,000 prize to the person who would circle the globe in hours instead of days.

The inevitable Bilko scam emerged: Ernie would con one of his air force buddies and have himself labelled 'Priority Emergency Baggage'. This would enable him to use military planes to circumnavigate the world in record time and walk off with the twenty grand. Of course, as in every script, capricious providence refused to co-operate and the 'priority baggage' tag ended up on a twelve-year-old boy.

Phil Silvers had appeared in Mike Todd's musical *Up In Central Park*, and Hiken and Silvers figured that it would be a stroke of showmanship to get Mike Todd to play Mike Todd.

I still have a clear memory of the film producer striding into Nola Studios, polo coat slung over his shoulders, Borsalino hat at a sharp angle, puffing a giant cigar. I muttered to Henshaw: 'I can't stand a cigar that's taller than I am.'

Mike took a huge puff of cigar and said in a loud voice: 'How many people watch this show?' Hiken answered: 'Thirty-five million.' Todd looked out of the window at the marquee of the Rivoli Theatre directly across the street where *Around The World in Eighty Days* was playing. 'Thirty-five million? Even if it's only twenty-five million it can't hurt the box-office. I'll do it.'

Hiken explained the story line and the mechanics of the show. When Todd heard that the *Bilko Show* was a three-camera shoot in front of a live audience he shouted: 'What kind of a schmuck do you think I am? Mike Todd is not going to make a fool of himself in front of a live audience. We'll do it Hollywood-style, like a movie. One camera and plenty of takes.'

If you want Mike Todd, you do it his way! Hollywood-style! The day of shooting arrived and Todd made his entrance – pure Hollywood-style. His retinue included a chauffeur in full livery, his lovely Chinese secretary (who, after Mike Todd's death became secretary to Mike's son, Mike Todd, Jr) and on his arm one of the most alluring women on earth, Liz Taylor, wearing the longest sable coat in the history of man.

Suddenly, the scruffy rehearsal studio took on a glow fuelled by all the glamour and by the way Liz and Mike looked at each other. Watching them, we all felt that Mike Todd was truly the love of Elizabeth Taylor's life.

Mike Todd was a great showman but, let's face it, he was no actor. When the actual shooting began, Todd showed a unique talent – he blew every line! Every once in a while he would look towards Liz and call: 'Sweetheart, how'm I doing?' Liz would answer: 'Marvellous, wonderful.' No matter how badly he massacred his speeches, Liz would beam as if he were Laurence Olivier.

The great impresario kept fumbling the dialogue until Phil Silvers said: 'Come on, Mike, pay attention.' Mike Todd, jokingly, said: 'Listen, last time I paid attention, I went bankrupt.' Phil, always quick with a retort, said: 'That's what you're doing to us. We're running into overtime.' Finally, a desperate Hiken said: 'It's a wrap.'

Before the Todd entourage even reached the front door, Hiken was already whispering to Silvers: 'We'll use him in the opening and in the closing and forget about him the rest of the time.' And I thought to myself that having a Rolls Royce was status, having a chauffeur to drive it was necessary, having a Chinese secretary was exotic, having a glamorous star as coach and wife was incomparable. But all of these gratifying perks are no protection against a pair of scissors and the absolute power of the final cut.

Mike Todd may have not been much of an actor but he was a creative producer, a relentless promoter and a mensch,[1] as I discovered some years later when I was in Israel. My wife and I were Sabbath guests of Meyer Weisgal, the director of the famed Weitzman Institute. In an earlier life, Weisgal had been a Broadway producer and so the talk turned to showbusiness. Weisgal told us that when *Around The World in Eighty Days* premiered in Israel, Todd promised that the profits from the film's

---

[1] A Yiddish word, now part of American English, that means a person who has admirable characteristics.

engagement would go to the State of Israel. (Israelis, by the way, are among the top moviegoers in the world.)

Shortly after Mike left Israel, he was killed when his private plane crashed in bad weather. Some time later, Elizabeth Taylor was invited to Israel to receive an award. Weisgal was at the function and he mentioned Mike Todd's promise to donate the profits from the picture to the State of Israel. Liz smiled: 'I heard Mike say that and since it was his wish it's also mine.' It's nice to know that in the Todd family being a mensch was contagious.

Following the Mike Todd episode, when Silvers and Hiken realised that filming movie style, without a live audience, reduced the pressure on the performers, they decided to go that route. There was also an important fringe benefit. Those in the company, not in the scene before the camera, could participate in a marathon nickel and dime poker game that started Monday morning and ended Friday evening. Silvers, ever the big gambler, boasted: 'I don't play for nickels and dimes.' So I said: 'Phil, on the set when the camera is rolling you're a star. Out here you're just a foot soldier.' Our leader knew how to be gracious: 'Deal me in, after all this is the only game in town.'

I never dreamed that Mike Todd's appearance on the *Bilko Show* would not only change the way the cast worked but would also be of profit to me. Filming Hollywood-style, despite the advantages in production, left us with a programme without audience reaction – no laughter and applause on the soundtrack.

One day I was summoned to the office of the executive producer. Executive producers, despite the title and the corner office, are essentially keepers of the budget. For instance, if the plot calls for a wedding they will tell the writers: 'We don't want anything lavish with second cousins and friends. Keep it down to the immediate family. Better yet, have them elope.'

This was the first time I had been called for a face-to-face with the master of the finances and I have to admit that I was nervous. An actor is always insecure. On the way up to the office I kept mentally rereading my contract. Since I was the shortest man in the platoon I worried that maybe they had changed the height requirement or maybe they wanted me to chip in for cleaning and pressing my uniform.

Much to my surprise, the EP was very cordial. He said: 'Mickey, we need your help. CBS has figured out a way to add audience reaction to the show. They want to screen each new episode before a live audience. The applause and laughter will be recorded and combined with the soundtrack. Since you're a stand-up comedian, we want you to warm up the audience and explain what's happening.'

So, every two weeks, I and an army captain who had been assigned as a consultant to the show would take two episodes to Governor's Island where they would be screened for the military and their wives.

As I recall it, my seven- or eight-minute warm-up went something like this: 'Good evening ladies and gentleman, I'm Private Fielding Zimmerman, a member of Sergeant Bilko's motor pool. I'll be showing you the most recent episodes that we have filmed. If they're funny – laugh. If they're not funny – laugh. CBS was going to send a Vice President down. But most of them are very tall and, if they have to fall on their knees and beg, it's a long way to go. But for me, I'm already halfway down. I could have been tall – but I turned it down. In fact, it's good to be short – when it starts to rain you're the last to know.'

By this time the audience started to loosen up, so I

would continue: 'I'm glad you're such a good group because it's been a rough day for me. When I got on the subway this morning a madman got on behind me. I knew he was mad because he kept yelling: "I'm George Washington, I'm George Washington." People on the subway were scared but I kept my cool. I yelled: "Next stop Valley Forge." He got off.'

A solid laugh. Time for me to wind it up: 'I was just offered a new show – a quiz show – bigger than Twenty One or the Sixty Four Thousand Dollar Question. The grand prize is a million dollars. We give you the questions and answers – you have to guess who sent it in. Oh by the way, did you hear about the woman on that quiz show. They asked her: "Under history, for ten thousand dollars, who was the first man?" And she said: "I wouldn't tell you for a million." '

My closing line was usually something like this: 'If you don't laugh these will be the most expensive home movies ever made. Roll the film.'

But they did laugh and their laughs were recorded and incorporated into the release prints.

This routine was very funny in 1957. These days the world has changed, tastes have changed and the standards for comics have drastically altered. We live in a time when we're supposed to let it all hang out and a four-letter word has to be part of every punch line. But I think an audience today would still laugh at that innocent warm-up routine. As Phil Silvers used to say: 'Funny is Funny.'

One day the consultant captain confided to me that he was having trouble with his back and that he was thinking of leaving the army. He was hoping that CBS would keep him on in the same capacity. Six weeks later he turned up on the show as the civilian military consultant. Since he was no longer in the army, Hiken was able to use him as an actor – an MP, a security guard, a jeep driver. It was not until he won the Academy Award years later, for *Cat Ballou*, that I realised how great he was in those simple parts.

When the series ended after programme number 142, the ex-captain felt that he was a bona fide actor and so remained in showbusiness. Had this captain had the same drive and ambition in his military career he would have ended up as a four-star general. The captain's name was and is George Kennedy. These days, George has been winning acclaim as Leslie Neilsen's right hand man in the *Naked Gun* series.

Around this time, CBS put on an hour-and-a-half *Bilko* special that ran on a Saturday night. It was sponsored by the makers of Pontiac cars. In addition to the platoon and Silvers, it featured many star names, including Sid Chaplin.

Many other people on the show went on to great fame . . . others to notoriety. David Beigleman, Phil's agent, approached me and said: 'Freeman, I hear you're doing a good warm-up routine for the audience at the laugh-track sessions. I'd like you to do the warm-up for the special.' I was pleased at being asked, but honour was not enough. After all, CBS was paying me substantially for doing the sessions on Governor's Island. I told David that I expected to be paid for the additional work. Beigleman was a tough negotiator and we haggled back and forth and finally agreed on a price.

We did the special, I did a fifteen- or twenty-minute well-received warm-up and forgot about it until the cheque came in – no extra money. When I spoke to Beigleman about it, he said: 'Look at the fine print in your contract. Any actor can be called upon to help introduce the show.' He completely ignored the fact that we had made a deal. I went to SAG, the Screen Actors' union, and complained. They felt that I had a good case but they advised me not to antagonise Phil Silvers' agent. In the long run, fighting a man in Beigleman's position could cost me a great deal more than the reneged fee. I forgot about the incident until years later, when David Beigleman had become president of one of the major Hollywood movie studios.

One day Beigleman was a lead story in all the media in the country. He had been caught forging the signature of an expense cheque of ten thousand dollars. The story unravelled in the next few weeks, and it turned out that he had been using the studio's finances as a personal bank account. He was fired and subsequently committed suicide.

When the stories about Beigleman's financial machinations appeared, I thought to myself that cheating me out of a few hundred dollars, all those years ago, probably was just a tryout for future larcenous actions!

6 Actors Are Made Not Born

Forty years after the final episode of the *Bilko Show*, the producers of the successful movie *Apollo Thirteen* decided to go from men in outer space to men who were spaced-out. They made a film called *Sgt Bilko*, starring Steve Martin and Dan Aykroyd. Before filming began, a copy of the screenplay was sent to the Defense Department in the hope that it would induce the military to permit the production to use army bases and equipment in the making of the new Bilko saga.

To the consternation of the movie company, the brass turned them down cold with words to the effect that the army is made up of brave, young soldiers, not men who run dog races. In fact, the closing credits for the 1996 film read: 'No Thanks to the United States Army for its lack of cooperation.'

How unlike our situation in 1956 when the army was delighted with our concepts and scripts and arranged for Captain George Kennedy to be assigned to our set as technical consultant and liaison.

These days it seems that everybody wants to be a performer – stage, screen, TV. Many of the best universities offer schooling and advanced degrees in the thespian arts. In every part of the country, apprentices to summer productions and small theatre companies are to be found learning the craft. TV commercials feature astounding four- and five-year-olds whose diction is perfect, whose reading of lines has a genuine spark and whose facial expressions have star-like qualities. These young people acquire their professional abilities very young. Parents have been using TV to mind the baby and baby is a keen observer and a fast study and has a very big hard disk – he or she remembers everything. These are the ways that actors are being created in this high tech era, but it was not quite that easy in the *Bilko* days.

One of Nat Hiken's great talents was spotting people who had the face and voice he needed. He could ferret out perfectly innocent civilians who had never dreamed of being on TV and make them into credible performers. One of Nat's better efforts as Pygmalion was turning Jack Healy into the platoon's Private Mullin.

In his youth, Jack was a rough guy with tough connections. His contacts enabled him to become the manager of a jazz club on 52nd Street and somehow he became friendly with Rocky Graziano, an up-and-coming fighter from the Lower East Side. Healy realised that Rocky had the makings of a champion and brought him to the attention of the 'right people'. The 'right people' did right by our Jack, and they rewarded him with a small interest in Rocky's contract. Rocky became one of the great fighters of all time and went on to win the championship in his division as well as the respect and admiration of everyone around him.

Rocky was a sweet, gregarious man. He appeared on radio and TV and the better-mannered talk shows of his day. His big performing break came when Nat Hiken, who was then producing the *Martha Raye TV Show* on NBC, hired him as a regular for that programme. Rocky was an instant hit and he and Nat became firm friends. When Hiken was casting *Bilko* and looking for original personalities for the platoon, Rocky introduced him to Jack Healy, who had done many things in his checkered life, although acting was not one of them.

One of his ventures had changed his life forever – he became involved in the numbers racket. (Even though 28 states now have legal Lotto games, private enterprise in that era was and is frowned upon.) One day Jack's luck ran out and he was arrested in a police raid. He and his lawyer managed to get his trial postponed month after month, until an exasperated judge ruled that Jack had had his last deferment.

Jack was a man with a real zest for the better things of life, particularly when it came to eating the finest Italian dishes and drinking the best wines. Prison fare was definitely not his dish. When he realised that he had run out of legal strategies, he looked for a ruse to further delay his trial. He persuaded one of his friends, a prominent doctor, to put him in the hospital for fictitious 'stomach complaints'.

The hospital staff read the chart and proceeded to give him all the tests a genuine patient would have had to endure. Jack reckoned that an enema was a small price to pay for a chance to keep himself out of the slammer. Some days later his lawyer informed Jack that the scam had worked and another postponement had been granted. The very next morning Jack asked for his clothes and was ready to sign himself out when the doctor in charge came in and protested: 'Mr Healy, you can't leave. You're a very sick man.' Jack said: 'Doc, I feel wonderful. The only complaint I have is the hospital food. I can't hang around any longer. I have a date with a dish of osobucca.' The doctor said: 'Jack, I have to give it to you straight. You have cancer of the intestine.' Jack replied: 'Hey Doc, you must be reading someone else's

41

chart. I can't have the big "C".' But, finally, the doctor convinced Jack that he really was in danger.

They operated and removed a yard of cancerous gut. After Jack's recovery he had to appear for his long-delayed day in court and his lawyer explained his medical situation to the judge. A compassionate man, the judge ruled: 'Mr Healy, you have cancer, God has punished you enough. Case Dismissed.'

Shortly after Jack's illness, Hiken hired him to play the part of Private Mullen. It turned out that his cancer made the difference between an extended tenure as a guest of the government and a long-term contract with CBS.

Jack, who had never performed before, turned out to be the consummate professional. He always knew his lines, delivered them well, and was a genuine asset to the production.

Another civilian Hiken turned into a military thespian was the good-looking Walter Cartier. His appearance added a great deal of class to the platoon. Although not an actor, Walter was used to performing in public. He was a boxer who was a contender for the welterweight championship. He was just a punch or two away from the title but he realised that he lacked the killer instinct and gave up boxing.

Walter played Private Claude Dillingham. He was a gentle man as well as a gentleman. His brother was an assistant DA in Brooklyn. He was married to a lovely woman and she and their children were thrilled that Walter was leaving the dangers of the ring. They were all proud that he had found his way into the exciting world of showbusiness.

For years, Walter and I were comrades in the *Bilko* army and good friends in real life. One week at the Monday rehearsal Walter, who had not fought a professional bout for a number of years, announced that he had been booked to fight a four-rounder at St Nick's Arena which, in those days, was second only to Madison Square Garden as a boxing venue. So we realised that this was an important contest and Walter's opponent had to be a very good fighter.

It went without saying that all the members of the cast would show up at the arena to root for our friend and colleague. We were certain it was going to be a festive evening. The night of the fight all of us were settled into ringside seats. After all, we were the *Bilko* platoon.

When Walter was introduced we led the cheers so that he got an energetic reception. If boxing matches were decided by sound levels, Walter Cartier had won his fight by a vocal knockout. But then reality set in, as our Walter's opponent kept landing devastating punch after punch. Unlike other boxing matches we had witnessed, we felt each blow and almost physically shared our friend's pain. When Walter lost the fight we understood that we had not been just onlookers – we had been participants. But our sadness was as nothing compared to the anguish of Walter's wife.

At the next rehearsal, when a somewhat battered Walter announced that this really had been his last fight, the platoon cheered and gave him a standing ovation.

It occurs to me that boxers and actors are very much alike – if you don't work regularly at your craft, you wonder if you've lost it. When a boxer is losing, you can see the bruises and the blood. When an actor is losing, there are neither bruises nor gore, but it hurts just as much.

Acting was not in Bernie Fein's career plans when he left upper New York State to tackle the Big Apple. The young man was a friend of the super-press agent, Eddie Jaffe, who allowed him to sleep in his apartment. This was the same apartment that Hiken and Silvers used as an office in the daytime when they were working on ideas for a *Phil Silvers* series. Thus, Phil, Nat and Bernie were casual acquaintances. As Silvers and Hiken left for the day they would pass Bernie coming in to spend the night.

When Nat needed an actor to fill out the platoon he felt that Bernie could play one of the parts. He dubbed him Private Gomez. This served a double purpose – it gave Nat another character and it took Bernie off the unemployment line. Bernie was Gomez for the run of the show and, since he was always in the back rows of the formation, I dubbed him the 'Unknown Soldier'.

When the show finally went off the air, the 'Unknown Soldier' achieved some recognition, at least among some of the people in the business. Bernie took to writing and selling television scripts. Interestingly, in most of his scripts he kept reinventing the *Bilko* platoon. A year or so after the *Bilko* series ended production, I was cast in a show with Lloyd Bridges in a script written by none other than Bernie Fein. In this show, a baseball team was the platoon. Sometime later I heard that Bernie had sold a series to Bing Crosby Enterprises that became a major success – *Hogan's Heroes*. Once again the platoon format appeared.

When I met Bernie and asked how he had achieved such a coup, he explained: 'The first setting for my show was in an American prison camp. No sale. I tried using a French prison camp. Still no action. Then I revised the script to a British prison camp. No deal. In desperation I set the show in a Nazi prison camp.'

That clinched the deal. Bernie was riding high as creator, associate producer and part-owner of the property. One day, the people who produced *Stalag 17*, a play about a prisoner-of-war camp which had been big on

Broadway, sued Bernie Fein for plagiarism, claiming that the premise for *Hogan's Heroes* was the same as the one for their play.

When the case came to court the judge ruled against Mr Fein, and Bernie's bubble burst. Jack Healy's and Walter Cartier's stories had happy endings, but poor Bernie Fein's did not. Nat Hiken proved that he could take a handsome near champion fighter, a wise-guy with street smarts, an incipient TV writer who had never been closer to Broadway than Albany and make them into solid performers. But he needed an eclectic mix of personalities and talents to flesh out the platoon and create what, these days, is called diversity. Much of the cast was hired the traditional way through agents and casting calls, the tyros bonding together with the professionals in a platoon so authentic that we almost believed that it really existed.

Nat and Phil regularly chose many splendid, seasoned professional performers to fill out the cast. These included Paul Ford, Allan Melvin, Harvey Lembeck, Billy Sands and Nicholas Saunders.

Paul Ford played Colonel John T. Hall. He was forty years old before he was offered a paid acting job – at three dollars a week! Even in those post-depression days it certainly was not enough to support five children and an uncomplaining wife. His wife was used to Paul's thespian ambitions – she shook her head and said nothing. The children didn't mind – according to Paul they thought everybody ate only peanut butter sandwiches.

Paul's finances had been touch and go for years as he struggled with many jobs. He wrote short stories, was a nightwatchman and had his own catering service. He had gone to Dartmouth University and was on his way to becoming either a journalist or a lawyer, but he became neither when his father's business crashed and he had to leave college.

After years of trying every kind of show business, Paul's burning desire to be an actor was finally fulfilled when he got a small part on a radio soap opera. His talent was quickly recognised and soon he was performing in fifteen radio soap operas a week – at union scale.

Because he came to acting late in life, Paul had not developed the facility for quickly learning new material. Consequently, he often went up on his lines. Since the show was filmed as if it were live, Silvers had to rescue him with an ad lib time after time. Phil maintained that he was entitled to an award for working with Ford.

Paul was appearing in the Broadway hit *Teahouse of the August Moon*, starring David Wayne. Broadway tradition had always been that when the star first appeared on stage he would get a tremendous round of applause. Paul Ford was playing a secondary character and got little audience recognition. However after the *Bilko Show* had been on the air for two months, David Wayne would come on and receive a big burst of applause, but when Paul came on the house came down. Such was the power of TV and the *Bilko Show*.

Paul Ford's motion pictures include *The Matchmaker*, *Perfect Strangers*, *Advise and Consent*, *It's a Mad, Mad, Mad World* and *The Russians are Coming*. His stage credits include *Teahouse of the August Moon* and *Music Man*.

Allan Melvin played Corporal Steve Henshaw.

He was appearing on Broadway in the hit show *Stalag 17*, when Hiken saw the play and raised Al's rank to Corporal by hiring him for the *Bilko* series.

He was an extremely quick-witted man. One day we were out to lunch and as Allan watched Maurice Gosfield eating and decorating his clothes with food, he said to Hiken: 'Nat, I think we should get stunt pay.'

Allan John Melvin was born in Kansas City in 1923. He started as an impressionist and won the *Arthur Godfrey Talent Show*. He appeared in the Broadway production and touring company of *Stalag 17* and had running parts on *The Dick Van Dyke Show, The Joey Bishop Show, Gomer Pyle*, the *Bill Dana Show, Green Acres* and the *Andy Griffith Show*. He created the roles of Sam the butcher on *The Brady Bunch*, and Barney on *All in the Family* and its spinoff, *Archie Bunker's Place*.

Allan did voices for many cartoons and also did voice-overs for numerous commercials. His biggest account was a product called Liquid Plummer, which he worked on for fifteen years.

Luck determined that on the very same day that the *Bilko Show* was cancelled, Allan's long running commercial should also be terminated. Poor Allan – out of two lucrative jobs on one day.

In the list of credits he sent to me, Allan includes this item: 'Happily married to the same lovely girl, Amalia, for 52 dynamite years.'

Harvey Lembeck played Corporal Rocco Barbella. In the early days of the show the recognition it brought Harvey was extremely rewarding but, as time went by, he became frustrated as he realised that his superior acting talents would not be fully used on the *Bilko Show*.

After his stint on the *Bilko Show*, Harvey appeared on Broadway and then moved to Hollywood where he acted in more than thirty films. He opened a very successful school for comedy, which is still operated by his daughter. His son is Michael Lembeck, one of television's leading comedy directors. Sadly, Harvey died of a heart attack when he was very young.

In theatre, he appeared in *Mister Roberts, Stalag 17, Wedding Breakfast, Oklahoma* and the touring company of *Man of La Mancha.*

Harvey's many films included *You're in the Navy Now, Stalag 17, Love with the Proper Stranger, The Unsinkable Molly Brown, How to Stuff a Wild Bikini* and *Raid on Entebbe.*

As for television, Harvey appeared on many, many shows from 1955 through to 1980 including *The Goldberg's, Hallmark's Kiss Me Kate, Ensign O'Toole, Please Don't Eat the Daisies, All in the Family* and *Love Boat.*

Billy Sands played Private Dino Paparelli. Back in the late 1930s he was a member of the prestigious Broadway theatre company The Group Theatre.

In addition to being a fine actor, he was also an excellent Borscht Circuit comedian in New York's Catskill Mountains for many years.

After *Bilko* went off the air, Ed Montagne, the producer, found himself unemployed in Hollywood. One day Universal Studios asked Ed to look at a pilot of a TV show they had made starring Ernest Borgnine. Universal asked if he could make a comedy out of their pilot. Ed said: 'I immediately visualised *Bilko* at sea – the navy with a bunch of funny sailors. Bingo – another hit.' The studio immediately bought his ideas and over the next few weeks they kept pressing for the names of the cast.

Montagne went to New York to get away from the studio pressure and to make contacts for cast members. He ran into Billy Sands on Broadway and told him about the plans for the new show. It was the end of June, and on 1 July Billy and his wife Marcia were booked for eight weeks at a Catskill resort where Billy was the comic and director of activities. Billy was just about to get in the car to go to his summer job when he heard the phone ringing. He went back to the house and it was Ed Montagne offering him the role of Tinker in *McHale's Navy*.

Billy spent four years in Bilko's army and another four years in Borgnine's navy. That's what I call a uniform life.

On Broadway, Billy appeared in *The Rugged Path* starring Spencer Tracy, and *Make Mine Manhattan* starring Sid Caesar.

On radio, Billy was a regular on *Milton Berle's* radio show, which Nat Hiken wrote and produced, while, on television, he starred in *McHale's Navy*.

His films include *How to Frame a Figg, Evil Roy Slade, Rocky, Raid on Entebbe* and *High Anxiety*.

Nicholas Saunders played Captain Barker. He was born in Russia in 1914, but did not begin his acting career until the 1940s. His father was an important stage actor in the Soviet Union. The family escaped to Shanghai and then was able to enter the United States.

When a *Bilko* script called for a second-in-command, Captain Barker was always on the roster.

Nick was not only a very talented actor, fate was also good to him. Paul Ford had the lead in a Broadway hit show *Never Too Late*. When Paul took the production on the road for a year, he left Captain Barker in charge of Fort Baxter. Barker became Bilko's new patsy.

In recent years, Nick translated Chekov plays from Russian into English. One play was such a hit in California that he was invited to bring it to London.

Nick and his wife Greta were good friends of ours. They had lived in the same New York apartment – nine rooms on New York's West Side – for something like forty years. When they left to live in California it was a great personal loss for Anne and me. With the exception of myself, Nick Saunders was the last vestige of the *Bilko* platoon on the East Coast.

During the four years of making the *Bilko Show* it was sometimes difficult to separate fiction from reality, and we often called each other by our character's names. The line between actuality and play-acting was so tenuous that my mother used to refer to herself as 'a dependent of Pvt Fielding Zimmerman'.

7 The King of Chutzpah

A man named Hubell Robinson, a renowned CBS VP, was responsible for bringing the talents of Phil Silvers and Nat Hiken together, a happy marriage of which the *Bilko Show* was the pampered offspring.

Phil used to say: 'When the world sees a television show, they see only the tip of the iceberg.' And in the candid and intriguing autobiography he wrote with Robert Saffron, Silvers explains how it all came about. Phil was appearing in *Top Banana*, which was a tremendous success at the Winter Garden Theatre on Broadway. On a Sunday night, in those days, Broadway was dark, so he was able to do a 'command performance' at the Mayflower Hotel in Washington. As Phil tells it, President Eisenhower, Vice-President Nixon, members of the Warren Supreme Court, senators, congressmen and cabinet members were present. Missing only was the famous Secretary of State, John Foster Dulles, who was in Europe on a mission.

The secret service was nervous about the fact that so many top-level people were present. A terrorist incident that evening could literally shut down the United States. Security even turned off all the telephones in case the ringing of an instrument was used to detonate a bomb.

When Phil came on stage and looked around at the

entire administration in one room, he said: 'Who's minding the store?'

Later, as Phil Silvers was performing, playing his clarinet, suddenly off in the wings a telephone rang. Secret service agents rushed to get to the phone. The audience, understandably, tensed up. But Phil, the showman, kept his cool. He walked calmly to the wings, nodded and walked back to centre stage. He looked up at the box where Ike was seated and said: 'It's from a Mr John Foster Dulles. He'll talk to anybody.'

Hubell Robinson, who was in the audience, was so impressed by that brilliant ad lib that he came backstage and suggested that Phil do a TV series. Phil, who had been warned by his friend Jack Benny that TV was an all-consuming monster, refused. But Robinson was persistent. After a number of weeks he once again contacted Silvers: 'Phil, I'll get Nat Hiken to create a show for you.' Nat Hiken was the magic name that moved Phil from the stage to the tube.

For a year, Phil and Nat worked together in press agent Eddie Jaffe's apartment on 48th Street. They experimented with many formats until they came up with the concept of Sgt Bilko.

Being a star of his own television show was a new experience for a man who had done everything else in show business. His career actually started in a local movie house in Brownsville, Brooklyn. The nine-year-old Phil, who stole fruit from pushcarts, vandalised buildings and shoplifted at the dime store, was on his way to becoming a juvenile delinquent. The proceeds of his 'criminal activities' enabled him to see the silent movies of the day. These pictures were accompanied by a lady on an asthmatic organ who played mood music as the plot unfolded. One night, the film broke and while it was being repaired, the young Phil decided, on his own, that he would fill the void with his spontaneous rendition of a popular song of the day. After a few seconds the organist joined in and when the song ended and the applause erupted the boy soprano's future was sealed. Pleasing the crowd was more satisfying than fleecing the crowd.

Fishel (later Phil) Silvers was the son of Russian–Jewish immigrants who had brought him to America at an early age. There were six boys and two girls ensconced in two bedrooms. His father was an ironworker on the skyscrapers then being built all over the city. His job was to catch the rivets that held the steel girders together. These red-hot missiles were flung by the man at the furnace to the catcher who fielded them with a tin can. It's quite possible that Phil's steely nerves were genetic.

In the early part of the century the ironworkers in New York were mostly Irish. Phil writes that his father, an orthodox Jew, spoke English with a unique accent. Today it might sound like a fusion of Jackie Mason and Barry Fitzgerald.

The Silvers lived in a tough neighbourhood. The streets were controlled by a bunch of hoods called by the newspapers 'Murder Incorporated'. An important member of the local mob was a man for whom Silvers worked many years later in Las Vegas – Bugsy Siegel. The streetwise kids on the block quickly learned not to call Mr Siegel 'Bugsy' to his face.

In order to survive in the Silvers' neighbourhood, a boy had to be a street warrior. Phil writes that he did not have the stomach for gang fights – but he did have the tongue to talk his way out of brawls. The King of Chutzpah had started his reign.

Decades before the 'Actors' Studio', Phil devised his own method of acquiring professionalism. He took his courses at the Bushwick Theatre, a local vaudeville house which featured headliners such as Belle Baker, Sophie Tucker, George Jessel and Ted Healy. He memorised their routines, their jokes, their facial expressions, their body language. Most of all, he learned their songs. The ambitious young man heard that beer halls could be a starting point for novice talent. No formal pay, but a note well sung was sometimes rewarded with bank notes from the appreciative audience. Sometimes! But mostly they threw nickels and dimes.

From beer halls to kiddy shows was a logical step for a ten-year-old and eventually Phil began working for Gus Edwards. Edwards was the impresario of an important vaudeville act called 'School House Revue'. The careers of stars such as Ray Bolger, George Jessel, Eddie Cantor and Walter Winchell started under his tutelage. At an early age, Phil became a genuine pro – with a regular paycheque of $75 a week, which was big money in those days.

Soon after his thirteenth birthday, disaster struck – Phil's high soprano voice started changing and he was advised not to sing for at least a year. It was a difficult time for Phil as he watched himself grow taller and more awkward – a young man used to a weekly paycheque with no job in sight.

A famous vaudeville team, Campbell and Morris, needed someone to play the son in their act. Joe Morris recalled seeing Phil with Gus Edwards and contacted him, offering him the role. This was Phil's first experience reading lines.

After a break-in period the act shaped up and was good enough to be booked into New York's Palace Theatre (arguably the best vaudeville house in the world). Phil remained with the act for six years. He was making two hundred dollars a week, but the job was frustrating. Here he was, six feet tall, twenty years old and still playing a kid in short pants. When Silvers asked for a rise, he was fired.

Despite having made a good income for many years, Phil was broke. Many years later he explained it all to me. He said: 'When it came to money I was just a middle man. My family and the bookies never went hungry.'

Around this time, Phil met Herbie Faye. They did an act together and, more important to the two men, a friendship was founded that lasted all their lives. Herbie was a brilliant technical comedian – double takes, triple takes, slow burns. Phil was like a sponge and absorbed all these skills. Phil never forgot a comic technique.

When he appeared on Broadway in *Top Banana* he hired Herbie Faye to play the hilarious part of the barber. When Phil became Sergeant Bilko, Herbie was his stand-in and also played the important role of Private Fender.

To get back to 1929 – the act that Herbie and Phil was using was not really going anywhere. All they could get were bookings in second-rate vaudeville and burlesque houses, and they decided to give the act up.

It was summer and Phil knew that there was work to be had in the Catskill resorts. The Catskills are a range of mountains in the middle of New York State, the locale of Washington Irving's 1820 story of Rip Van Winkle. And in the middle of the twentieth century they became famous for a seemingly endless supply of resort hotels frequented by up-and-coming members of the Jewish community of New York City.

These establishments featured non-stop activities and food that was both traditional and inexhaustible. Because of the cuisine the area was called the 'borscht belt'. As jet travel became ubiquitous and the cost of going to 'far away places with strange sounding names' became accessible, ordinary people used their summers to broaden their horizons instead of their abdomens.

Today, those Catskills hotels still operating feature top-money headliners: Alan King, Buddy Hackett, Shirley McLaine and other stars of that ilk. But back in the 1930s and 1940s, a performer was hired to be on staff, one of a group of talented people who lived at the hotel from 1 July until the first week of September.

Performing was only a small part of their responsibilities – they were on call day and night to amuse and coddle the guests. Their duties included running potato races, playing 'Simon Says', falling in the pool fully clothed and, let's not forget, dancing with the ladies, both single and married, at night.

The centre of all these activities was in a special building called the Casino, a structure that had absolutely no connection to gambling. Anyone who has ever worked on the staff of a Catskills hotel can recite the schedule: Monday – Game Night; Tuesday – Champagne Night, a dance contest where the winners received a bottle of bubbly (I was always suspicious of the quality of the prize since the bottles were labelled 'no deposit, no return'); Wednesday night – Mid Week Review; Thursday – Amateur Night (when I was on the staff, I used to say that the twentieth century had endured three great disasters: the San Francisco Earthquake, the sinking of the *Titanic* and Amateur Night in the Catskills); Friday – Dramatic Night; Saturday – The Weekend Review, the culmination of seven days of creating scripts and music, set building, costume fabrication and rehearsing (whenever the tired staff was not involved in its many other functions); Sunday was Introduction Night, when new guests were introduced to everyone on the staff, from the chef to the boy who was in charge of the rowboats.

Phil acknowledged that a lot of the keen sense of timing and instantaneous ad libs came from those summers in the mountains.

During the years of the *Bilko Show*, I worked most weekends in the Catskills. Come Monday rehearsal, Phil would want to know where I had performed, and one time I reported that I had been at Brickman's. 'Brickman's,' said Phil, 'I remember the owner, Murray Posner, who turned me down for social director because I wore glasses and my face was not the kind that would be attractive to the single ladies.'

One Monday morning I told Phil that I had appeared at the Young's Gap Resort. He said: 'Sit down Zimmerman. I was the social director at that hotel. On the 4 July weekend we were rehearsing our big holiday show and I was looking for a big finale. I came up with a great idea. I sent the property man out for a bushel of apples and I felt that we were set for the evening. Come show time and the finale, the girl singer comes out and sings "An apple a day keeps the doctor away". She throws apples to the audience. The baritone sings "An apple a day keeps the doctor away". He throws apples to the audience. The dance team, the straight man, the bandleader all follow suit. Then I came out and sang the magic words and threw my pieces of fruit. By that time the audience was well armed with apples, and they began throwing them back at the cast as they chanted "An apple a day keeps the doctor away". Audience and cast were soon involved in "The War of the Apples". We were able to keep the doctor away but not the State Troopers who had to be called before peace was restored.'

One of the people Phil met in the Catskills was Jack Albertson (who later won an Academy Award for *The Subject Was Roses*) and they put an act together for burlesque. Burlesque was an art form that had its own special niche in New York and other big American cities. The shows featured gorgeous striptease artistes and skilled comics who were, by and large, masters of their profession. The Minsky Brothers were the kingpins of the burlesque circuits. They owned theatres in many parts of the country and were well respected for their honesty and showmanship. Their presentation of near nudity was another question, one that brought them into conflict with the local authorities.

The Minskys bought the Silvers–Albertson act. Eventually Albertson left to pursue his straight acting career, but Phil remained in burlesque and became the outstanding star of the Minsky circuit. The flagship Minsky theatre was the Gaiety on 46th Street and Broadway, right in the middle of the theatre district where some top producers and directors became aware of Silvers' dazzling comedic talent.

Hy Gardner, a well-known columnist, recommended Phil for a small part in a show called *Yokel Boy*. Phil always felt that he read badly at auditions and asked if he might ad lib the lines of the character for which he was trying out. He was brilliant and got the part. The money was far less then he was getting in burlesque, but it was Broadway!

The show was not a success, but Phil came off with great personal reviews. Phil Silvers had turned a minor stage role into a major success – sufficient reason for MGM to sign him to a movie contract.

Phil's early Hollywood career consisted of performing at parties in the homes of the stars, doing benefits and special events. He was a smash – but no one cast him in a picture. His paycheque came in every week and his life was pleasant – but boring. Phil was the toast of the town, but man does not live by burnt bread alone. To be happy you have to work at your craft.

One Friday night, Silvers was invited for dinner at the beach house of his boss, Louis B. Mayer, a man who had defined the phrase 'movie tycoon'. The evening had been set up so that all the MGM department heads could meet the newly contracted talent. Naturally, they called on Phil to perform and he did twenty hilarious minutes. He broke up stars, directors, writers and producers and left them weak with sustained laughter. When the laughter and applause had died down, Mr Mayer stood up and, according to Phil's book, said: 'You all seem to be thrilled by this young man. I signed him personally. I didn't know he was so versatile. All of you had notification about him but somehow none of you have seen fit to use him. Aren't you ashamed?' Mr Mayer's generous words had an immediate effect, and first thing Monday morning Phil's option was cancelled!

The other Hollywood companies were not as reluctant as MGM to use Phil's exceptional talents and there were lots of roles for him. During his Hollywood days, Silvers did many pictures. Phil claims that he played the same part in film after film – a role called, generically, Blinky. Blinky is always the best friend who gets the laughs but never the girl.

During his Catskills period, Phil had made friends with Sammy Cahn, the great lyricist. Sammy was working with Julie Styne on a Broadway musical called *High Button Shoes*, and he offered Silvers a part in the show which starred Nanette Fabray. In part, because of Silvers' witty ad libbing and hilarious performance, the show became a major success.

When Phil was in a Broadway show, everyone brought money to the bank – except Phil. Broadway or Hollywood, Phil was an equal opportunity loser. He could gamble away huge amounts of money on the East Coast as easily and frequently as he did on the West Coast.

Top Banana was Phil's biggest Broadway hit. In it he played a comic modelled after Milton Berle. It was not exactly a flattering portrait since it satirised Berle's consuming interest – Milton Berle. One day he met Berle at the Friars, and Uncle Miltie wanted to know what the new show was about.

As Phil describes it, he did not want to offend his good friend, so he said: 'It's about a guy who's been "on" all his life. His only goal is to get laughs. He never listens to anyone because he's always thinking of his next gag line. The guy never gives himself a chance to acquire knowledge about people, politics, art or how to be generous.' After a long pause, Berle commented: 'I'll be a sonofabitch. I know guys just like that.' Berle became the show's biggest booster and bought two backers' units.

On Broadway, Phil was on a winning streak. Every night he tried to keep the winning streak going with an all-night poker game at the home of a famous show conductor, Ray Bloch. The game would start at 11.30 p.m. and last until 11 o'clock in the morning. No time for fancy dining, visiting with friends, enjoying the fruits of his success. To top it all, his impatience made him a bad poker player and he nearly always lost. But those night-long card games served to push away, for a few hours, the depression and insomnia that had begun to plague him.

Top Banana was a great stage show, but when it came to movie rights the world-class con man was conned by a producer of B pictures. As usual, Phil was desperate for money, and the producer gave Phil 25 per cent of the anticipated profits. The arithmetic is simple – 25 per cent of nothing is nothing. The producer's hustler's cinema technique consisted of pointing a camera at a simulated stage performance of the show – no close-ups, no expanded views, no artful photography. The total shooting schedule for a major Broadway production was less than two days, and the result was disaster. Phil had lost big again, and it didn't help his depression.

The call from CBS giving him the go-ahead on the *Bilko Show* took him off the couch and put him back on his feet, both emotionally and financially.

Everyone in the *Bilko* cast was aware of Phil's gambling addiction, but we never knew the extent of his winnings or losses. During the *Bilko Show's* summer hiatus, Silvers was booked for a month at the Sahara in Las Vegas. Salaries have always been huge in Las Vegas, but with good reason – many of the performers give it all back at the gambling tables.

One year, just before the TV show went back into production, I ran into Phil outside Lindy's. Phil said: 'Zimmerman, have you had lunch?' It was the first and last time I heard those words come out of his mouth. Normally, Phil's money was not for lunching, but was reserved for gambling. At lunch I asked about his affair with Lady Luck in Vegas. Phil said: 'She was no lady. The first three days were sensational. At every show I had standing ovations before, during and after. I was so busy taking bows I had no thoughts of gambling. But on the fourth day I ran into Danny Thomas outside the hotel. Danny said: "Phil, how're you doing?" I replied: "We're a smash. We're killing them every night. I'm having so much fun that I've stopped gambling." And Danny said: "I can't believe that you're not playing. Gambling is therapy. We work hard all year round. You come out here you have to give vent." '

Phil was easily persuaded and suggested some places where they could challenge the house, but no matter what hotel he mentioned, Danny turned it down. They finally wound up at the only resort in Vegas where Danny Thomas' credit had not been choked off. Danny

Thomas and Phil Silvers at the same crap table was a major tourist attraction. Phil told me: 'In twenty minutes I was out 2,800 dollars. This was before the first show. I figured that after the show I would recoup.' Phil continued: 'But it didn't work that way. I kept losing and telling myself that I would break even, beat the house, break the bank. But what really happened was that I was wiped out. Four weeks of losing a lot, winning little and the score was: Silvers zero, Vegas 140 grand.'

That number was exactly his salary for the month. Out of that sum he had to pay the cast, travelling expenses, hotels and let's not forget the IRS. Anyone who has ever read a balance sheet knows that this was a case of Situation Impossible.

After the 142nd episode, Phil was called in by CBS and told that there would be no more new *Sgt Bilko Shows*. These days, TV producers know that original episodes of a show can be syndicated at the same time that new episodes are being created for the network. The new shows increase viewing figures of the syndicated programmes and syndication increases the number of viewers tuning into the new episodes. But, back in the 1960s, CBS was under a lot of pressure to put the *Bilko Shows* into syndication – a move that promised them great profits. The thinking of the brass was that additional episodes on the network would reduce the syndication value of the *Bilko* series.

In addition to receiving a generous cash settlement, CBS sweetened the pot by giving Phil a production company, which he named Glad To See Ya, after his trademark line. When Sherwood Schwartz came to CBS with the premise for *Gilligan's Island*, he was told that CBS would finance part of it and suggested that the Phil Silvers production company would undertake the rest of the financing.

Years later, when the *Bilko* contract ran out, he had little chance to work. Phil's living and medical expenses were astronomical and it was the income from *Gilligan's Island* which kept him going through those lean times. Sherwood Schwartz told me that Phil's profits from *Gilligan's Island* exceeded the total of all the money he had made in his entire professional career – including the *Bilko* earnings.

In Phil's relationship with women, chutzpah became charm. Both of his wives were beauty contest winners. His first wife had been a Miss America and his second wife, Evelyn Patrick, had won many beauty contests and was under contract to Revlon. Her commercials ran on the famous show *The Sixty Four Thousand Dollar Question*.

Evelyn was not only a beauty but also a sweet, caring woman. She and Phil had five children, all girls. The way Phil explained it, every time he said 'Hello Honey' too loudly he had another child.

After *Bilko* filming stopped, Phil starred in a Broadway show with Nancy Walker, called *Do Re Mi*. He made some movies and then returned to CBS with *The New Phil Silvers Show*, but it barely survived its thirteen-week guarantee. Not too long after that, Phil showed signs of depression, both emotional and financial. The mental depression showed itself in physical ways – unexplained illnesses, the shakes, palpitations and sudden sweats – and if this were not enough, Phil developed a cataract in the left eye. He went to Spain to film *A Funny Thing Happened On The Way To The Forum*. Suddenly, he had little sight in the left eye and lost his depth perception, which handicapped him terribly. But the trouper in him prevailed and he finished the picture.

When he returned to Hollywood the cataract was operated on and his sight was fully restored. But his depression kept getting worse and he ended up being treated by psychiatrists.

One day, Larry Blyden hired him to star in a stage revival of *A Funny Thing Happened On The Way To The Forum*. During the rehearsals for the show a joyous thing happened to Phil – his seven-year depression suddenly lifted and he returned to being the Phil Silvers of old. The reviews in New York were ecstatic and he received the Tony Award as the best actor of the year.

On 31 July 1972, Phil suffered a minor stroke, forcing him to withdraw from the show and closing the production. He made a good recovery, but the movers and shakers of show biz were leery of him. Between tough-minded insurance companies and timid producers, no one wanted to risk hiring Phil Silvers.

Phil's anger at the tycoons of his industry was monumental. His frustration was saddening to all of us who knew him and worked alongside him. In a telephone interview from California to the *New York Daily News* he lashed out. The headline of the piece read: 'Phil's Willing to be a Second Banana'. What a devastating comment coming from the lips of America's Top Banana.

In that interview, he said: 'I'm the best comedian in the country. I do more interviews for TV and radio on the phone than anybody else. But all on the phone, why don't they put me on the air? I'm sitting here in this phony town with all the directors and producers and production companies and nothing. I had a stroke but I'm fully recovered. I did six shows on Broadway, every one a hit. With me comedy is no laughing matter. I made that line up myself.' The chutzpah had turned into bitterness.

At some point in 1984, while at the California Friars Club, I heard that Phil had had a second stroke. He had stopped coming to the club and even refused to come to the phone. I called him. The phone was answered by a woman, obviously a nurse. When she told Phil who I was, he came to the phone. His 'hello' tore into my guts – his voice was so weak, so sad, so pitiful. I told him that I had been doing a gig on a cruise ship and had ended up in LA. He said: 'You're lucky. The excitement is still in your voice and you're performing.' I said: 'Phil, I've just been in London and *Bilko* is still number one and you're hot in England.' Phil answered: 'You know, I've been withdrawn. I'll start to do my therapy and maybe I'll get better.' I said: 'Phil, we're counting on you. Get well.' He hung up and I cried.

On 1 November 1985, Phil Silvers died. This was the man who, as Sgt Ernie Bilko, gave international status to the art of chutzpah. In the college of con men he was the dean, an inspiration to every aspiring hustler. When the *Bilko Show* started I had seen Phil Silvers in many movies and had admired his hilarious professionalism in *High Button Shoes* and as the top banana in *Top Banana*. The character of Bilko was a combination of the many roles that Phil had played and of his personal life style. The sarge had two outstanding attributes: brass balls and the love of gambling.

We all knew that Phil was a gambler in real life, but I didn't realise how long he had been in training for this role. One night I was the after-dinner speaker at a fund-raising affair for a local charity in Toronto. When the toastmaster introduced me as Private Zimmerman of the *Sgt Bilko Show*, I received a standing ovation. 'Gentlemen,' I said, 'Wait till I say good evening.' A voice from one of the tables called out: 'It's not for you – it's for Phil Silvers.' From different parts of the room people shouted: 'Phil bought my wife a fur coat' . . . 'Phil sent my kid to college' . . . 'Phil paid the mortgage on my house'. I said: 'I never knew how charitable Phil was.'

And then I realised that these men were all bookmakers in Toronto. Years before the *Bilko Show*, when Phil was working in local burlesque houses, he would 'share' his salary with them each payday.

Although Phil gambled in his personal life, in his professional life he left nothing to chance. Because of his long years as a burlesque sketch comic, the sneaky smile, the charm, the facial tricks were as natural to him as a mumble is to a method actor. His timing was as precise as a quartz watch.

Every new *Bilko* script needed a couple of new actors, and the most professional of them would be nervous because the regular members of the platoon were like a well-rehearsed repertory company. Phil had a standard speech of reassurance for the newcomers. 'You're doing great. Just say it fast – say it funny.'

I've worked shows where a performer would get a big laugh in rehearsal. Come show time the laugh line was still there, but it came out of the star's mouth. In 142 shows, Phil never took a funny line away from another performer.

Phil Silvers died in his sleep. Had he been awake, I'm sure that he would have talked his way out.

WHAT SOME OF HIS FRIENDS SAID ABOUT PHIL SILVERS

Milton Berle:
Phil Silvers was my friend . . . but I'm only one among millions. Phil Silvers was a friend of the whole world, a recognisable face that people all over the globe identified with laughter. At this very moment, somewhere on the planet, some television station is showing Phil Silvers as the inimitable Sergeant Bilko, raising havoc with the military. The lovable con man character that

Phil created is being enjoyed in every country on earth. It is a universal source of laughter, and Phil Silvers was the driving force that made it so.

Phil was an original in the field of comedy, a dynamic artist who was honoured and respected by his peers. Among comedians, he was the complete professional – a master of timing with a superb delivery, a true perfectionist of his craft. That sly, silky, smooth voice, those black horn-rimmed glasses, the ingratiating manner and sincere grin that warmed the audience while it sucked them into his mischievous antics – all were trademarks of Phil's comedic technique.

He was not a stand-up comic but, rather, a fine actor who performed comedy with the best of them. Phil won four Emmys on television and was a Tony-winning entertainer on the Broadway stage, a hilarious performer who appeared in countless motion pictures, even a songwriter who produced one of Sinatra's big hits, *Nancy with the Laughing Face*.

The talent of this superstar will be sorely missed by all of us, especially his many pals at the Friars Club, his home away from home. Phil was a man's man who gloried in the world of male camaraderie. Give him a friendly game of pinochle or a fast filly at Hollywood Park. Phil's greatest pleasure was to wager a few bucks and root like hell.

Today, we are not here to mourn Phil Silvers. It is more important that we celebrate his having lived among us as a vital part of our lives. My memories of this multi-talented giant go back a long way. It was right after the World War I when Phil and I met as teenagers, two young hambones struggling to make it big in show business. Incidents and anecdotes by the score flash through my mind when I think of Phil but, so long as I can recall and relive these marvellous moments, he will always be with me. And the same can be said for every man and woman who ever shared a memory with him, whether a personal one, or as an image on the stage or screen.

And nobody shared more delicious memories than those who were closest to him – his beautiful wife Evelyn, his five lovely daughters, Tracy, Nancy, Laury, Cathy and Candy, and his darling granddaughter, the apple of his eye, little Jaclyn Sarah, who was named after his beloved mother.

We'll all miss him terribly, but we're deeply grateful for the legacy of laughter he left us.

The Top Banana has joined all the other top bananas. And I'm sure that somewhere up there, Phil is saying to Jack Benny, to Durante, to Cantor and Ed Wynn: 'Hi ya, fellas. Glad to see ya!'

God bless you, Phil, and thanks for your friendship and a million laughs.

Red Buttons:
Most of us in this chapel have known each other for a lifetime.

In the 1930s, when I dreamed about show business, I used to *shlep* downtown from the Bronx whenever Milton Berle or the Ritz Brothers played Loew's State. On one of those journeys, my youthful libido propelled me across the street to the Gaiety Burlesque. I went to see the dolls but I fell in love with a guy, comedian Phil Silvers, a love affair that's lasted all my life.

The cliché tells us that life is a gamble and that the cards are stacked against us. And that very few of us ever fill to an inside straight. Phil did – he took a comic spark and ignited it into a comic brilliance. He found what all great comedians have been able to discover in themselves – a rhythm of movement and speech that complemented their physical being. In Phil's case, it

translated itself into the charmer we all came to know as
Bilko. Phil, in his infinite comedic wisdom, was able to
put skin, bones and flesh on a hip hustler to a point of
making him laughable and lovable, a crucial prerequisite
for every clown.

This invention will serve as his monument to the fra-
ternity of all those who ever dared extract the elusive
prize called laughter from a faceless and oft-times hostile
audience. Week after week we watched with anticipation, glee and respect as this awesome comedy
machine demolished everything in its path – the raw
energy, the raucous verve and, let us not for a moment
forget, the native intelligence and street smarts that
comprised this one-man army.

It was nothing less than poetry in motion to watch Phil
as Bilko weaving his own special brand of magic. An
original at work. If he were a painting he'd be hanging in
the Louvre. Phil Silvers was a Top Banana. What else is
there to aspire to if you're a funny man?

Cindy Adams (columnist, *New York Post*):
In the early days, Milton Berle's mum Sadie (who in later
years, became Sarah) used to say to her Miltie: 'I want
you to hang out more with that nice boy Phil Silver-
smith.' And little Milton would say: 'Why Mama?' And
Sadie/Sarah would say: 'He has such nice pink cheeks.
He is such a clean-living boy.'

As Milton has told it over and over: 'You know where
that nice clean-living boy who was two-and-a-half years
younger than I, took me? To my first house of ill-repute.'
It was in Phil Silvers' will that Milton do his eulogy.
Milton was in Denver doing a concert, but flew to LA
especially for it.

Philly, as we all called him, was a man's man. He
loved being with the guys. He called them all 'Pal', as in

'How are ya'pal.' His ex-wife Evelyn Patrick, a beauty who had been on *The Sixty Four Thousand Dollar Question*, bore him a house full of daughters. But Philly had a baggy-pants comic's heart and, rather than an evening with his wife, he'd sit and throw the bull. Better still, he'd prefer to throw a card.

Philly made it the hard way from top banana in burlesque to Sgt Bilko on TV, but he blew it all at the card table and crap tables. If it had been his to give away, he'd have laid his whole series on the hard eight. Years and years back, when he and my friend Evelyn were breaking up, we'd talk a little bit about it. He loved Evelyn, but luck was his lady. One day we were discussing the fact that Howard Hughes, who owned hunks of Las Vegas, never left his room. And Philly cracked: 'If I did that in Vegas I'd have money, too.'

He was often out of cash, but never out of jokes. One night our phone rang. Late. Maybe two in the morning. A normal time for saloon prose. He called from Vegas to talk to Joey. (Cindy is married to comic Joey Adams.) Phil said: 'It's Philly pal.' 'Yeah, Philly, what is it?' asked Joey. Phil replied: 'I'm in Caesar's. They even got slot machines in the men's room so that you can get washed up and cleaned out at the same time.' Then he slammed down the phone and went back to the crap game, and we sat up the rest of the night.

In 1954 when Milton was king of TV, Silvers got his own weekly show. Nat Hiken, he told us all, was going to write it, and CBS was giving him the 8 p.m. spot opposite Milton. Milton screamed: 'Listen, 111 shows who went against me already have been knocked off. You'll get killed. Nobody goes against me and the Texaco Show and lives.' Fade out, fade in. A year passed and so did Silvers.

He passed right by Milton in the Nielsen ratings and his *Sgt Bilko* was the hottest show on TV.

The eulogies by Milton Berle and Red Buttons and the column by Cindy Adams were reprinted from *Ye Epistle*, the magazine of the Friars Club, January 1986.

8 Funny Things Happened on the Way From the Typewriter

The term laid-back was invented to describe Nat Hiken. Had he lived in today's world, people would have compared him to a computer nerd. No one would suspect that from this low-key writer would come such high-class comedy.

Common wisdom has it that, as a class, comedy writers are brilliant ad libbers, witty, spontaneous and, in their everyday life, devisers of hilarious practical jokes. Always on! And, without notice and just a dab of make-up, they can step in front of an audience and do twenty boisterously entertaining minutes. Common wisdom is often wrong.

This popular notion is true for less than a handful of professional laugh-makers. Most of the creators of comedy save their great lines for the typewriter or computer keyboard. Their wit and creativity really flourish on paper.

Nat Hiken was such a writer. Give him a small room, a manual typewriter, an urgent deadline and in a few hours he would produce an award-winning script. At least that's the way the cast of *Bilko* thought about their multi-talented leader. But Alan King, who was an intimate of Nat's, gave me a fresh slant on the Hiken sense of humour. 'Back in the fifties I had a three-week engagement at the Eden Roc Hotel,' said Alan. 'Miami at that time was one of the great entertainment centres of the world. Friends and colleagues threw lavish parties nearly every night and always invited my wife Jeanette to keep her entertained while I worked.

'When the job was over I wanted to reciprocate by doing something special. So I rented a city bus complete with uniformed driver. I had an on-board bar set up and hired three violinists. I took 36 people on the most involved progressive dinner in history. Seven courses, each in a different restaurant.

'One of my guests was Nat Hiken and as we were driving down Collins Avenue toward our last stop, Hiken turned to me and said: "Let's have some real fun. Dim all the lights and pull up at the next bus stop."

'A woman was waiting for the bus. She boarded and we could see she was an attractive lady. She wore a nurse's uniform with "Ruth" printed on the nameplate. Without noticing a thing she dropped her fare in the box and walked to a seat. As the bus rolled away the bright lights came up, the violins began to play and a couple started to dance in the aisle. Ruth's face showed bewilderment. "Would you like a drink," I ask her. She says: "Aren't you Alan King? What's going on?" Nat Hiken, with a straight face, said: "Mr King has been hired by the city of Miami to host a special bus party as a promotion for public transportation."

'Without batting an eye our only fare-paying passenger said: "In that case I'll have a scotch and soda." She had three drinks and forgot about getting off at her stop, so we had the driver take her right to her door.

'I still have nightmares that somewhere there is a woman who has been committed to an asylum because she claims that she was at an all-night party on a Miami City bus. Alan continued: "Had there been credits at the end of the bus trip they would read: Written and Directed by Nat Hiken." '

There was more to the story. A couple of years ago I was reminiscing about the old days with Alan King and I brought up the tale of the 'Fiddlers on the Bus'. Alan asked: 'You never heard the sequel to that story?' When I shook my head, Alan continued: 'Some years after the incident I told the story on the *Johnny Carson Show*. Soon after the broadcast I received a letter. The writer said: "Bless you, Alan King, for telling that story on *Johnny Carson*. I was the woman on that bus and when I talked about the festive vehicle that served liquor on the streets of Miami, everyone would shake their heads and roll their eyes, as if to say 'There she goes again' with her fantasy. Thank you Alan King for validating my sanity." '

Phil Silvers said that Nat had the most fertile TV comedy mind of the 1950s. Indeed, *Time Magazine* polled comedy writers in 1956 and Nat Hiken was voted the 'finest comedy writer in TV'. However, looking at some of the *Bilko* episodes in 2000, Phil's opinion might be amended to 'the most fertile TV comedy mind of the second half of the twentieth century'.

The many burdens of writing, producing and directing the *Bilko Show* week after week soon overwhelmed Nat. When he realised that he could no longer carry the creative chores alone, he brought in a number of other writers, including Neil Simon, Coleman Jacoby, Arnie Rosen, Barry Blitzer, Terry Ryan, Leonard Stern and Joe Stein. These talented people point out that Hiken was not only a great comedy writer, he was also a superb re-writer who added much to their scripts in both plot and dialogue.

I came from a family that spoke and read Yiddish and in my home we considered the brilliant humorist, Sholom Alechim, unequalled as a comic genius because of his wonderful stories and novels about the Jews of Eastern Europe. One of his novels, *Tevye The Dairyman*, was the basis of the musical *Fiddler On The Roof*. American Jews frequently compared Alechim to Mark Twain. (Mark Twain, when he was introduced to the Jewish writer, graciously said that he, Twain, was the American Sholom Alechim.)

Nat also came from an immigrant family that held Sholom Alechim in high esteem. His father, uncles and grandfather not only loved to tell their own stories, but would also regularly read Alechim's works aloud to their enthralled kin.

Hiken's TV episodes did not depend on jokes and one-liners. Character and situation and the twist and turns of an amused fate stimulated the laughter. To those of us in the know, a script by Nat had the subtlety and tongue-in-cheek humour of a Sholom Alechim short story.

Since man took sharpened stick to clay tablet there have been two kinds of writers – the organised ones who write for a specified number of hours each day and deliver their work on time, and then there are those who cannot set a word down until an irate master, high priest, publisher or theatre manager stands over them screaming for their text. When it came to procrastination, Nat was a gold medallist. He was unable to write until a deadline stared him accusingly in the eye. Then, and only then, would he sit down and in a few hours turn out a script that would take a good professional comedy writer a week or ten days to complete.

Nat had planned to be a journalist and he studied the trade at the University of Wisconsin. But winning a Pulitzer was not as important to him as the sound of other people's laughter. He wrote a humour column for his college newspaper and produced and wrote a radio show called *The Grouch Club*. His next move was a major one – he joined the writing staff of one of the top-rated network programmes, *The Fred Allen Radio Show*. In his early days, the much-admired Allen created all his own material, but performing and writing a high-powered radio show week after week all by himself proved to be an impossible task.

Eventually Allen hired four bright young comic minds to help him, and he soon recognised Nat's genius and made him the leader of the pack. Nat did a fantastic job as head writer, but most of the public still believed the myth that Fred Allen wrote all his own material. After Nat had worked for Fred for seven years he decided that the time had come to seek new stars and fresh laughs. Mr Allen never forgave him for leaving his show.

Nat became the head writer for Milton Berle's radio programme. Week after week the keen lines rolled out of his typewriter creating waves of audience laughter and much appreciation from 'Uncle Miltie'. Berle then moved over to TV comedy, an art form which he and other professionals invented and reinvented week to week. TV was new and exciting and attracted some of the best show-biz minds of the era. However, like the producers of silent films who felt that talking pictures were only a fad, Nat was certain that TV would never supplant radio. Nat remained true to his first love and was involved with several important radio series for a number of seasons.

When he finally did face up to changing times and took on the challenge of cameras, lights and sets, it was as the writer–director of the *Martha Raye Show*. He moulded the exuberant, free-form Martha into a polished TV comedienne and taught Rocky Graziano, the boxing champion and non-actor, how to deliver a funny line.

Sitting at the manual typewriter, Nat was an outstanding creator of mirth. Standing on his feet in the studio he was an equally outstanding comedy director. He came up with great lines and wonderful 'shtick'[1] in seconds. As an actor I was always aware that some very funny things could happen on the way to the camera. For example, one script called for Bilko to walk into Lindy's Restaurant. In the revolving door a startled woman tourist is supposed to look up and say: 'Phil Silvers?' As the scene was about to be shot and the actress had actually entered the door, Hiken called out: 'Make that Sid Caesar.' On the air, that bit drew tremendous laughs.

Professionally, Hiken was the most secure man I ever met. I recall, with much pride, an incident that happened on the fifth or sixth show. Hiken passed me holding a script. 'Zimmerman,' he said, 'How do you like this line?' I read it and replied: 'Nat, it's funny, but I'm sure you can come up with a better one.' Nat mumbled something and went on his way. Hours later a line came to me and I tried it out on Nat. To my amazement, he turned to the cast and said: 'Ladies and gentlemen, Mickey Freeman has just come up with the end of the show.' Of course, I was gratified. In a business that's as much ego as talent, it's rare to find producers, directors or writers who acknowledge an actor's contribution. After that, Nat often kibitzed me when I was involved in a behind-the-set card game saying: 'Why are you wasting time – we need a line.'

Hiken knew and cared so little about the technical aspects of TV production that Al DeCaprio was listed as the show's director and Nat was given credit for staging the production. I recall Al coming over to Nat and asking for a retake on a short scene because the lighting was not

---

[1] A piece of comedy business.

quite perfect. Nat put his arm around A1 and said: 'Al, did you see the guy come in the door, did you see the girl go out the door, did you hear the laugh – that's about as much light as we need.'

Hiken was a kind and generous man. Maxwell House Coffee had offered me a half-hour afternoon TV show that would be on a local station every Tuesday afternoon at noon. I asked Nat about the proposal and told him that I could be back at rehearsal by three. Nat said: 'Take it. We'll work around you.'

So every Tuesday about three I would come into the Nola Studios carrying the suitcase that contained the clothes I had worn on the local show. Quietly, I would set it down, pick up a script and casually drift into the rehearsal. Nobody seemed to notice.

One week, because of traffic, I came into Nola a little late. Nat caught sight of me and, sounding angry, asked: 'Where were you Zimmerman?' Flustered, I replied: 'It's Tuesday, Nat, and the traffic was terrible . . . I didn't realise I was needed.' Nat said: 'Who needs you . . . we needed the valise.' And I said: 'This is the first time in my career that I've been upstaged by a piece of luggage.'

Compared with most TV productions, the *Bilko* set was a sea of calm friendliness – temperament, jealousy and inflated egos were not to be found. But behind the scenes, some strains existed. Recently, I visited Red Buttons in his Bel Air home and he told me about a phone call he had received from Hiken as the first season of *Bilko* was coming to an end. Hiken told Red that Silvers had demanded a tremendous rise for the coming season, and the network wanted to know if Red would be interested in taking over the role of Sgt Bilko. Red said: 'Thanks Nat, that's very flattering but give Silvers whatever he wants. He is Bilko and Bilko is Silvers. There can be no one else.'

In the middle of the second season, Nat Hiken was showing more and more strain from his multiple responsibilities. One Monday, when we were assembled to read that week's script, Nat introduced us to Charles Friedman. I recognised Friedman as the director who had recently done *Ruggles of Red Gap* as a TV special. Nat informed us that Charlie would be directing our show. It was a shock. By now most of the cast believed that they were real soldiers, so it felt as if our general was handing over his command to a new and strange officer.

The next day, when we reported for duty at the rehearsal studio, we were astounded to hear our new director define our characters, explain our motivations and reactions to Bilko's scams. We had been playing those parts for two years and we didn't need explanations of who we were. After all, we had helped create our parts. The platoon exchanged puzzled looks but being in the military we followed orders. On Tuesday and Wednesday, Charlie staged the show, and Nat came in to observe rehearsals on Thursday. Nat sat next to Charlie, creating his own visual art from the tinfoil of cigarette packs. Any time Nat was under pressure he folded paper and foil into all sorts of animals and birds, a sort of stress-induced origami.

Nat watched us as we went through our paces. In less than five minutes, he got out of his seat and said: 'Excuse me, Charlie. Zimmerman, why are you standing at the foot of the bed? You never stand there. Move up.' Three minutes later, Nat again: 'Excuse me, Charlie. Paparelli, look to the left, not to the right.' Another couple of minutes and this time Nat leaped to his feet and there were no more 'excuse me Charlies' but an immediate restaging of the entire show. In thirty minutes, Nat undid a week's work and recreated our familiar image.

Friedman lasted for two more weeks. Because he was

such a decent man, a few of us took Charlie to lunch before he left. He summed up his brief tenure on the *Bilko Show* by saying: 'Gentlemen, take my advice. Never be a vice-president.'

Friedman's short-lived assignment proved that Hiken could not delegate authority. But with something as complicated as a TV show, you can't wear all the hats – writer, producer, director – and the platoon watched with compassion as Nat burned himself out.

Nat's search for a director continued. There was a young writer, Aaron Ruben, who had been doing good work on a number of radio and TV shows. Nat felt that Ruben could be a good comedy director and if need be could come up with some funny lines while the show was in rehearsal.

Aaron showed up one day and I recall how unsure he looked in front of the platoon. Recently, he told me that his first contact with us was a very scary moment. I went out to lunch with Ruben that first day and assured him that all the guys felt that he was the right man for the job.

When we were doing final revisions on this book, I went through my files for the tenth time to make sure I hadn't missed any mementos of the Bilko days. Sure enough, I found an overlooked newspaper page scrunched into a corner of the cabinet. It was seriously brown and terminally deteriorating, so I patched it together with scotch tape and imagination.

My archeological find was a page from the *World Telegram* (an important New York paper now long defunct) dated 29 November 1957, featuring an interview with Aaron Ruben, written by William Ewald, a staff writer for The United Press. Aaron and I had remained good friends ever since the Bilko days and I called to ask him if he remembered the article. He had no memory of the

article and asked me to read it to him over the phone.
The article read as follows:

There was a party on the set of the *Phil Silvers Show*
and everyone was out of uniform. Nineteen filmed
shows were finished and a six-week vacation had
been declared.
Everyone was feeling pretty loose.
Over at the buffet table, Pvt Doberman was
making eyes at the food. Sgt Henshaw, clutching an
empty glass, was negotiating a refill. Pvt Zimmerman was entertaining an appreciative audience
with an impromptu routine.
'Look around at this bunch,' said Aaron Ruben,
director of the CBS series. 'What a wonderful bunch
to work with. They get along with each other, they
work well together. But you know when they
offered me this job last summer I had real doubts
about working with this group.'
'There I was stepping into the shoes of Nat Hiken
– the creator, writer, producer, director of the show.
He had decided to pull out and it's no secret there
was trepidation all around. Who could follow
Hiken? He's the greatest, a genius.'
'What's more, I had never even directed before.
I'm a comedy writer – I've worked for the big ones,
Caesar, Berle, Burns and Allen, Sam Levenson,
Danny Thomas. But Phil thought my background
was an advantage. He felt that the kind of guy they
needed was one who had appreciation for a script,
who knew comedy.' He recalled with a shudder that
getting up in front of the Fort Baxter crew was like
plunging into icy cold water.
'Resistance? No, you couldn't say that there was
resistance to me. But let's put it this way – these

guys had been turning out one of TV's most successful shows for two years and they were out to size me up.

'By the end of the first two weeks I knew I had made it. And later I learned why I had made it. It was because the guys in the show began to sense that I knew the value of the platoon. That I knew it wasn't just a star show.

'Phil is a brilliant performer. He illuminates everyone around him. He's fantastic. He sets the pace of the show. But what the viewers probably don't know is the balance that the platoon members add to Phil's brilliance. And when they realized that I saw it – that I wasn't out to smear somebody, we were in.

'You know the secret of the show?' asked Ruben. 'I'll tell you. It's that we knock off sixty pages of script in 25 minutes. That's quite a clip.'

That yellow, crumpled newspaper story proves that Nat Hiken was not only a creative genius – he also knew how to choose his successor.

As well as writing a show from beginning to end, Nat was just as able to write a show starting at its end and working back to its beginning. This was proved in the writing of the episode that featured Bing Crosby.

Phil Silvers and Bing Crosby were both on the same *Ed Sullivan Show*. Nat came by on the Sunday afternoon to watch the rehearsal and when he saw the great Crosby he whispered that he had a script that would suit 'Der Bingle' perfectly. Phil knew that Crosby was a big *Bilko* fan so he asked one of America's most loved performers if he would appear on one of the shows. Phil was very casual about the invitation because he never dreamed that Bing would have the inclination or the time, but he accepted with three words: 'Where and when?'

This was Sunday and the time for shooting was set for the following Tuesday morning. When Phil and Nat left the rehearsal, Nat made a small confession – there was no script! But Bing had to have lines to read when he came to the studio. Without any idea of how the script would begin, Nat sweated out an ending. And so some sort of show-business precedent was established – an ending to a script that had neither beginning nor middle.

On Tuesday, Nat filmed a five-minute finale starring Bing Crosby. With that in the can, Nat worked backwards and wrote a show to lead into an already filmed climax. It turned out beautifully, proving that the astute Nat Hiken always got it right, coming or going.

Before the third season, Nat Hiken left the show and sold his interest in *Sgt Bilko* back to CBS. He went on to produce and write the *Car 54* series, which was saluted by the critics for its originality and for its true New York flavour. Ironically, it was the New York ambience that was the show's downfall. Unlike these days, Middle America was not interested in life in the big cities, so the show was not renewed for a third season. And it's that third season that enables a show to be profitable in syndication.

As an aside, during Hiken's administration of the show we never saw any network brass on the set and no front office directives came down to trouble the creative staff. Nat was in complete control. However, by the time *Car 54* went on the air, the climate had changed. Young, hungry network executives had started to make their weight felt throughout the industry as far as scripts and production were concerned. It was the loss of that complete control that upset Nat, and he started thinking about settling on the West Coast and doing movies. But before he left for the West Coast, Nat wrote and produced a *Phil Silvers* special for CBS. It was called *Phil Silvers in New York* and starred Carol Lawrence, Carol Haney and Jules Munchin. The Hiken touch was much in evidence in the brilliant satirical sketches the master of comedy wrote.

I remember one sketch in particular, a classic about the famed *New York Times* theatre critic, Brooks Atkinson, played by Phil Silvers. The sketch was introduced by the announcer saying that Brooks Atkinson had just retired from a long run as a critic. Age, explained the host, had nothing to do with Mr Atkinson's retirement. For years, Atkinson had been attending opening nights in the Broadway theatre district, which was confined to a few city blocks containing elegant theatres. In recent years, continued the host, off-Broadway and even off-off Broadway openings were now covered by the first-line critics in out-of-the-way venues. In the sketch the fictitious Atkinson and his wife are on their way to an off-Broadway opening night. Atkinson misreads the directions and instead of going down one flight of stairs he goes up one flight. The Atkinsons, in evening dress, find themselves in a lower-class apartment.

Assuming that this is the hard-edged realism of avant-garde theatre, they seat themselves on a couch in the living room. This is the home of the character played by the famous comedienne, Nancy Walker, with curlers in her hair, sloppy housedress, big shoes and bobby socks. Her husband, played by Lou Jacobi, is dressed in a disreputable T-shirt, stomach hanging over his belt, unshaven and drinking from a can of beer. Atkinson whispers to his wife: 'My God, what great characters.'

The 'on-stage' couple are arguing about their daughter dating a rich young man. They're not happy about him, their daughter and the entire situation. Suddenly, the door opens and their daughter comes in with her well-dressed boyfriend. As the young people enter, the Atkinsons applaud and the famous critic again whispers to his wife: 'Fantastic theatre – they bring you right into the action.'

Nancy Walker, for the first time, comes out of the kitchen and does a take when she sees the Atkinsons. She yells at her daughter: 'So you finally brought him home and I see you brought his stuck-up parents in their evening clothes.' The young man protests: 'These are not my parents.' The argument and the confusion reach a crescendo so high that the police arrive. At the fade-out the Atkinsons are led off in handcuffs.

The reason this brilliant sketch remains in my mind after all these years is that some time after it was broadcast I ran into Nat and complimented him on his satire. 'I'm glad you like it. I think you'll get a kick out of this.' He took a letter out of his pocket and handed it to me. It was on the real Brooks Atkinson's stationery and it said: 'Dear Mr Hiken, I saw your sketch about me on television and I certainly enjoyed discovering why I retired from the New York Times.'

Nat Hiken died of a heart attack in 1968. If Fort Baxter had not been merely a fantasy of his creative wit, the sound of taps would have been sounded for 'our general', the four-star genius Nat Hiken.

9 Show Favourites of Some Favourite Show People

Being a fan is one of the great human experiences. Participants in sports and the arts generate a special kind of loyalty and pleasure in those who follow their careers: a couple of unforgettable lines of Bogart's dialogue in a movie, an aria by Placido Domingo, the way Rembrandt painted light coming through a window, Pele scoring a goal, Sinatra's phrasing of a lyric. All great, unique, unforgettable moments. But television affords fans far more than just a moment as hit shows run for several years and create many episodes. So, aficionados don't have to satisfy themselves with just a few minutes of greatness, they can choose an entire favourite half-hour to store in their memory banks.

Some favourite show-business names have indicated their favourite *Bilko* episode.

Red Buttons:
I was a fan of Phil Silvers for many years, ever since the first time I saw him in burlesque as a teenager. We were friends, so when I heard that Phil was being starred in a new TV show, I made sure to watch.

As early as the second show, I was hooked. And it is that second show that's my favourite. It's called THE EMPTY STORE.

Sgt Bilko rents an empty store in town, and he makes

sure that the information is leaked to his fellow sergeants. The Electrical Sergeant Grover feels that Bilko has something lucrative going and asks for a piece of the action. Bilko mumbles something about an empty store. Grover buys one-third. The mess sergeant also wants in, and he gets a third. Sgt Pendelton the quartermaster also demands a share, and Bilko sells him the remaining share.

The three sergeants come in for a business meeting demanding to know what's going on. Bilko says: 'What do you want from me? You have a third, you have a third and *you* have a third. It's an empty store.'

I cracked up. It was a brilliant con flawlessly carried out.

These days they say that greed is good. But I realised back then that greed is *funny*.

Leslie Neilsen:

When the *Bilko Show* first went on the air I was a serious actor appearing on every dramatic show on the tube. I portrayed villains, heroes, romantic leads, winners and losers. Comedy was a thing I watched, not played.

When my friend Mickey Freeman told me that he was on a new show with Phil Silvers, naturally I tuned in. The brilliance of the material and skill of the star and the people who surrounded him struck me.

After the film *Airplane* I discovered that I could do comedy and it made me more appreciative of the writing and staging of the *Bilko Show*. My favourite episode was called DOBERMAN'S SISTER.

It was a yearly tradition at Fort Baxter that every soldier took out another soldier's sister, but every member of the platoon refused to consider dating Doberman's sister. Bilko convinces Zimmerman to date Doberman's sibling by quoting a law that he made up –

'Musselman's Law': 'The uglier the brother the prettier the sister.' It's a line that's stayed with me. Where other people rely on Murphy's law, my guru is Musselman.

Bilko is carried away by his own invention – Musselman's Law – and convinces himself that Doberman's sister must be a real beauty. He wants to be her escort, so he now tries to talk Zimmerman out of the date. He shows Barbella and Henshaw a picture of a famous race horse 'Man O' War' and tells them to let Zimmerman know that he has a picture of Doberman's sister. Zimmerman comes running into Bilko's office to find Bilko burning something. When Zimmerman asks him what he is burning, Bilko says that it's a picture of Doberman's sister. Bilko says: 'Did you ever see such ugly ashes?'

The entire show is hilarious, but it achieves a hysterical climax when Doberman, in drag, appears as his own sister.

Alan King:

As a monologist I've been making people laugh for many years. I walk out on stage alone, and it's just them and me. But an-act-in-one was not Phil Silvers' forte. He was a sketch comedian – not just great, but an original, a genius. He was a lovable con man so charming that at the end you found yourself cheering for the 'bad' guy.

Phil and I went back many years, professionally, socially and as Brother Friars. For Phil Silvers the transition from playing poker at the Friars Club to playing poker on screen with his fellow sergeants was an easy move. It just meant changing from civvies to a uniform. When the *Bilko Show* went on the air, I said to myself: 'It's about time the world got to see Phil Silvers.'

My favourite is the funniest *Bilko* show ever made –

THE COURT-MARTIAL, also known as the TRIAL OF HARRY
SPEAK-UP.

The army was instituting a speed-up for its recruit-
ment system and to accomplish this, short cuts were
made in the intake procedure. An organ grinder is called
up for military service, and he comes in with his chimpanzee. He explains that he has no place to leave it so
he brought it along to the induction centre. The chimp
escapes and lines up with the new recruits and in a
series of hilarious mishaps, the chimp is inducted into
the army.

Everyone feels that it would be quite an embarrass-
ment if the Pentagon found out that one of their GIs was
simian. The colonel rules that the only way to get the
chimp out of the army is to court martial him. The
chimp is charged with stealing bananas from the
kitchen, and Bilko volunteers to serve as the attorney
for the defence. Every time the prosecutor refers to the
defendant as a chimpanzee, Bilko jumps up and
screams: 'I object to having my client called a monkey.'
On screen we see Bilko whispering into the monkey's
ear as clients and lawyers often do during trials.

Nobody in the production realised that the chimp had
a thing for phones. In the middle of shooting the episode
before a live audience, the chimp reaches out, lifts the
phone and puts it to his ear. Phil makes what I think is
one of the great ad libs of all time. A beat, and Phil
casually remarks: 'He's calling another lawyer.'

At the conclusion of the show the army rules that it's a
hardship case and gives the chimp back to the organ
grinder.

If ever a show deserved to be in Television's Hall of
Fame, this episode was it. Ron Simon, the curator at the
New York Museum of Broadcasting, told me that THE
COURT MARTIAL was the most requested TV episode in

their collection. And as a postscript, I was told that just before the filming started, Hiken's secretary reached for the phone, the chimp bit her and she ended up in hospital.

Mel Tolkin (head writer for *Sid Caesar's Show of Shows and The Caesar Hour*, and story editor of *All In The Family*):
On the *Show of Shows* we created about fifty different characters for Sid to play and, with the help of costumes, props and special make-up, he was able to breathe life into each one.

Phil Silvers needed only a pair of glasses and chevrons to become the lovable con man who automatically made you check your wallet to see if it was still there.

I was impressed with Nat Hiken's ingenuity of plot and dialogue, and his skilful direction. I was also impressed with the way Aaron Ruben proved himself a worthy successor.

When I think of the *Phil Silvers Show* I think of an episode featuring the very funny Charlotte Rae. It was called THE TWITCH.

Gambling, as always, is a major problem at Fort Baxter, and Colonel Hall gets help from an officer's wife in trying to eradicate it. It seems she has a lecture about Beethoven which she feels is so powerful that it will distract the platoon from gambling.

When word goes out about her lecture, one of the men in another platoon recognises her and tells Bilko that she is known all over the army as 'the Twitch.' She had delivered this lecture at another camp and during her presentation she had tugged at her girdle 23 times. (This was in an era when all women wore girdles.) Bilko immediately perceives a gambling opportunity, and he sets up a pool for the entire camp. The object of the pool is to predict the number of times the lecturer will tug at her girdle during her talk. The closest guess is the winner.

I was impressed with the way the platoon was photographed for this sequence. You saw only the backs of heads as everyone watches the lecturer. Each time the lady tugged a chant went up . . . eight . . . nine . . . ten.

Cut to Allan Melvin broadcasting the event to the entire camp. 'She's up to seventeen and not even breathing hard', 'She's up to twenty-nine – a new world record.' Beethoven was deaf and so were the men to the lecture.

10 A Comic is Born

The editor of this book sent me an e-mail from London: 'Mickey, you've written about everyone else's life. How about yours? Not the life of Fielding Zimmerman but the life of the real Mickey Freeman.' A wise writer once said: 'Never question authority. A tough editor can do the story of your life and leave you out of it.'

I was born on New York's Lower East Side, birthplace of many famous show-business people: comics, actors, writers and songwriters – people such as George Burns, Eddie Cantor, Sammy Cahn, Lou Levy and many others.

My father was a tailor and my mother raised four children. My mother's family came from England. I was the youngest and the problem with having three sisters was that it was impossible for me to wear hand-me-downs. Both my mother and father were witty and had excellent senses of humour. Family legend has it that by the time I was two years old I was singing and dancing and seeking applause. My mother dubbed me a 'wise guy'. In those days, mothers were not sent home from the hospital eleven minutes after giving birth. Moms and their new offspring were given eight or ten days of hospital luxury in order to get used to each other.

My mother always claimed that on the third day of our hospital stay she was visited by a relative who sought out

the nursery, found my crib and cooed at me: 'And how old are you little baby?' I answered: 'Three days old.'
'And how did you get here?'
'My mother and father had relations and I'm the product.'
'You're only three days old. How come you know so much?'
I looked my questioner in the eye and said: 'I wasn't born yesterday.' As my young years went by most of the things I did and said confirmed my mother's prediction – I was, indeed, a wise guy.

We weren't poor, but we weren't well-to-do, either. When I was eleven or twelve I began to realise that if I could I bring in a little money it would be appreciated. I started doing small errands to earn tips and I let it be known that I was looking for after-school work. A neighbour told me that the local florist was in need of a delivery boy. I applied for the job, turned on my schoolboy charm, and I was employed. The salary was miniscule but the tips made the job worthwhile. Delivering bouquets and arrangements was not too hard, but one time I helped my boss deliver the flowers for a wedding and I was suddenly seized by a terrible sneezing attack. In those days who knew about allergies?

But what made me leave the floral business was when I had to deliver a funeral wreath at the home of the deceased. I brought in the floral tribute and the widow stopped crying long enough to say: 'Just put the flowers on the open coffin.' I had never seen a dead body and I was in such a hurry to leave that I forgot two things – I forgot to sneeze and I forgot my tip.

A few years later, as the school year ended, one of my friends said: 'I've got a job at a peanut stand in Coney Island. I can get you a job there.' I asked my parents and they were pleased that I'd be gainfully employed in the healthy ocean air. I'd also be exposed to the fun and excitement of the roller coasters and the crowds and jostling on the boardwalk.

In those days, Coney Island was a place for family excursions, hotdogs and hours of exposure to the rays of the sun. The measure of your pleasure was the shade of your tan – those were the good old days before sun block.

I got the job, but had to be to be trained in the intricacies of selling peanuts, Indian nuts and pistachio nuts. The sign over the stand was very large and proclaimed in huge letters: 'Peanuts 5 Cents a Pound'. Before the word 'pound', in very much smaller print, were the tiny numerals '$^1/_2$'.

Many times women would question me: 'This is not a pound – it feels more like a half pound?' Together we'd search for the $^1/_2$ on the sign. Pistachio and Indian nuts were five cups for a nickel. It looked like a great bargain, but close examination of the scoops we used would have shown that the bottoms of the cups were convex. I had to develop a technique of handing the bag to the customer by the top as I held the bottom so that the weight discrepancy was not noticed. This was my entrance into show biz – I was not doing comedy, but performing magic.

The owner of the stand had an original way of keeping books. He calculated his sales by the number of bags he gave us. Consequently, we would tell customers that we would give them some extra cups of nuts if they put them in their pockets rather than taking a bag. And many times when a customer would buy several bags one of us would follow him or her until he or she threw the bags away. We would recover them and reuse the bags. We were recycling paper before the planet even knew it had an environmental problem. It was youthful indiscretion, but profitable.

One customer went nuts about the nuts, or rather the lack of them, and started to pummel me. I yelled 'Hey Rube', the SOS of the carnival world. My distress call was quickly answered and six other young 'merchants' rescued me. After nearly being punched out I realised that the peanut stand job held a certain amount of danger, so I decided to look around for safer employment at the end of the next school year.

The next summer I became a barker for a small Coney Island bathhouse. A barker's job was to talk fast and convincingly. His patter would entice customers to the bathhouse where they could change into their bathing attire before going to the beach. Crowds would gather to listen to the spiel of a five foot one, fourteen-year-old kid who constantly slapped his hands together while intoning: 'Come on in, go bathing. Get your tickets here for the New Majestic Baths. New steam room, sun parlour, handball courts. Only 25 cents. Come in and go bathing.'

Our establishment was sandwiched between two large bathhouses, which had swimming pools. Would-be customers would inquire if we had a swimming pool, but I would avoid giving a direct answer. I would point to the ocean and say: 'All the water is out there. Come in, go bathing.' If my patter was fast enough, no one realised that I was not answering the basic question. The lack of a pool was the reason for our bargain price. The adjacent Washington Baths and Raven Hall Baths both had Olympic-size pools and therefore were able to charge 50 cents.

One day as I was 'barking', a young man approached me and said: 'Irving (my real name), I'm Dave Fisher' (real name David Fishkin). Dave Fisher had been director of activities at the Waldheim Hotel in White Lake, New York, in the Catskills. The hotel was next door to a group of cottages with a communal kitchen, where my family used to spend the summer. The custom those days was that the people renting the cottages would be permitted into the hotel to see the shows. Dave said: 'Do you still do your Eddie Cantor imitation?' I acknowledged that it was still part of my meagre repertoire. 'Come to see me next summer.' He gave me his card. He had an office on Broadway in the Strand Building, which was home to many theatrical agents. Before school let out that year I went to see him and Dave said: 'You're coming with me for the season. You'll be on my social staff at the Hotel Adler in Sharon Springs, New York.'

This establishment was a luxurious, six-storey brick building where people would come for the sulphur baths. The chemical smell permeated the entire hotel. The first employment of my life was in the flower business, a bad job that smelled good. Now I had a good job that smelled bad. But that's where I learned the ABC of comedy.

Dave Fisher was an agent in the winter months and a social director and comic during the summer. He had a collection of sketches and routines, which had been performed in burlesque and Broadway revues. He adapted them for our small company and I learned my trade by performing this material.

I was a quick learner, so much so that by the following summer I was able to become the social director at the Regal Hotel in Fallsburg. The Regal was not so regal – even on the postcards the beds were not made.

In succeeding years the hotels got classier, as I became one of the most sought-after comics in the Catskills. I always looked forward to Sundays when the people would check in. Sunday night was introductory night, and I would introduce and make comments about each member of the staff: the chef, the tennis pro, the head housekeeper. One line I used about those hardworking women was: 'This lady is one of our most trusted employees, especially since we found her stealing back towels from the guests. Management will be forever grateful.' When I introduced the bell captain I pointed out that he was also in charge of landscaping – wherever you saw an outstretched palm, it belonged to him. I felt that I had the Catskills in the palm of my hand.

I was looking for new territory to win when I came across George Scheck, an old acquaintance from the Lower East Side. George owned a dancing school in mid-Manhattan called the Ann Falk Studios. Ann Falk was his dancing partner and they had appeared in vaudeville together. George was considered one of the best white tap dancers in the business. He suggested that we team up and work the Catskills next summer. He would be in charge of the productions and I would be boss of the comedy.

In May we lined up the Hotel Plaza in Fallsburg and began hiring social staff which, according to Catskills tradition, would include a tall, good-looking male singer who would also be the comic's straight man, and a girl singer who could read lines. George and Ann were the obligatory dancers.

The following summer, George and I went to the Wald-mere Hotel in Livingston, New York. We had a generous budget, enough for a staff of nine people. We were a hit and the hotel brought us back for a second summer.

I'd like to digress for a moment while I tell you about the ways dancing schools operated in those days. George's school was very good and the teachers were excellent. But, in retrospect, I have to admit that his sales methods were, shall we say, unorthodox. A salesman carrying a clipboard with official looking papers would visit local apartment houses, knock on each door and ask: 'Are there any school-age children here?' In those innocent days the mother would invite him in and proudly introduce the child. The salesman would ask the child to show how high he or she could kick. No matter how high or low the kick, graceful or clumsy, the man with the clipboard would rave: 'A natural born talent. Ma'am we are prepared to offer you a scholarship. A free lesson at the Ann Falk Dance Studios.' Child and mother would come to the studio, where the sales pressure was turned on and the mother was convinced that the youngster should have private lessons.

In one Brooklyn apartment house, three separate children were offered 'scholarships'. In that same apartment house lived three prominent press agents: Si Rose, who was handling the nightclub The Hurricane, one of the biggest clubs in town; Art Franklin, who handled the Ink Spots and Robert Merrill; and Sid Garfield who, interestingly enough, was Phil Silvers' press agent.

The three mothers were a little bit wary of the 'scholarship' and asked Rita Rose and June Franklin if their husbands could check out the school that was in the heart of Manhattan. Instead of asking their husbands, Rita and June decided to investigate themselves and went to the dance studio. George Scheck was such a charming man that the two ladies enrolled in the school.

That summer, George was once again producing shows at the Waldmere. He suggested to Rita, his student, that if her husband Si could get a plug for the Waldmere in the New York City press, the hotel would give them a free weekend. Si wrote a fictitious release that said: 'George Scheck is producing a show written by comedian Mickey Freeman called *Honeymoon Hotel* at the Waldmere Summer Theatre.' The drama desks of all the New York dailies picked the item up and, of course, Si and Rita got their weekend.

The afternoon that the bogus story appeared in the New York papers, I got two telegrams, one from 20th Century Fox and the other from Paramount saying that they were interested in sending representatives to the opening of *Honeymoon Hotel*. Since the production was only the fantasy of a public relations man, Si and I decided that we had to be inventive.

I called the story editor who had signed the telegram for 20th Century and said: 'This is Mickey Freeman. I imagine you read about the fire at the Waldmere Summer Theatre. All the scripts have been burned and the production is off. I could, however, put together a short synopsis of the plot and send it to you.' She was very considerate and told me to send her the outline.

The lady at Paramount was even more sympathetic because the same thing had happened to her father, an author, who lost all his papers in a fire. She, too, encouraged me to send the synopsis.

Si and I, in less than three days, wrote a terrible film treatment. In about a week I received rejections from both film companies and between the lines I could read a subliminal message suggesting that we start a new fire.

The positive side of the story is that Si and Rita, Anne and myself became the best of friends, a relationship that has lasted more than fifty years, These days we sleep in Si and Rita's Palm Springs mansion and they sleep on Anne and Mickey's pull-out couch on 34th Street in Manhattan.

Subsequently, Si left press agenting and joined Bob Hope's staff as a writer, became Edgar Bergen's writer and then became the producer of *McHale's Navy* and the writer/story editor of the *Dukes of Hazzard*.

Sometime later, George Scheck called me and said he had an idea for a children's TV show and offered me the job of writer and associate producer. We had a sponsor even before we went on the air on a local New York City station, Channel 11. The show was such a hit that in a few months we moved to Channel 4, the New York NBC station. One of my producing duties was to audition the children who hoped to appear on the show and, one day, a young girl of fourteen came in with her father who was carrying an accordion case.

When I asked her what she wanted to sing, she started to unpack the accordion. 'No, no,' I said. 'Don't play. We're looking for singers.' She sang, accompanied by our piano player, and there I was listening to the voice that eventually sold millions of records. Her name was Connie Francis. I said: 'You're on the show.' A year later I left the show, but George Scheck had the foresight to sign Connie up and became her manager.

An axiom of show business is that a manager with only one star becomes a slave to the whims and desires of his client. Several years later, Anne and I were in Rome on the Via Veneto and came face-to-face with George, his wife Eleanor and young Barry Scheck who, many years later, achieved fame as the 'DNA' lawyer of the OJ Simpson murder trial. Connie was there doing an album for an Italian recording company. George complained that Connie insisted on eating dinner Rome-style, which meant at 10 p.m., much too late for young Barry and even uncomfortable for his parents. George said: 'I will tell Connie that I met you and we're going to have dinner together but you insisted that it had to be no later than 7.30.' At 7.30 we all met for dinner, and George had a surprise for us. He knew that it was our anniversary and, despite the fact that he spoke no Italian, he was able to get the maître d' to bring out a cake with candles. George Scheck really knew how to manage.

I had not seen Connie or George for a number of years when I received an invitation from George to attend a shower for Connie who was to be married. The suite at the Essex House on Central Park South, where the shower was held, was inundated with gifts, and Connie appointed me 'designated package opener'. With each package I opened I ad libbed a line or two, and my remarks got screams. And I began to feel that maybe package opening was a new facet of show biz for me.

The next day George called me and said that Connie was going into the famous Copacabana Night Club and that she wanted me to open the show for her. At the Copa they didn't provide packages. They expected a different kind of bundle – a bundle of laughs.

On opening night, rehearsal had just finished and I was sitting in Connie's dressing room, which was furnished with soft couches and drapes – elegance befitting a star. Show time was getting close and I went upstairs to my dressing room to find five black men getting dressed. One man said: 'Welcome. I'm Erskine Hawkins. This is my band and we're appearing in the lounge.'

That night my opening line was: 'The management here at the Copa has been fantastic. When I came into my dressing room there was a five-piece band – not playing, dressing.' I did twenty minutes and as I walked off to great applause, Jules Podell, the owner of the club, took me by the hand and led me into the kitchen. He turned to the help and said: 'What do we think of Mickey Freeman?' And in unison they all yelled: 'Hip. Hip hooray. Hip hip hooray. Hip hip hooray.' I was ecstatic.

I had just finished Sammy Davis' best-selling book *Yes I Can*. In it he said that the high point of his life was when Jules Podell took him into the kitchen of the Copacabana and asked the crew what they thought of Sammy Davis and they answered: 'Hip hip hooray.' Later, as I walked past Connie Francis' dressing room, she said to me: 'You're a hit. Jules took you into the kitchen.'

In retrospect, I have to admit that I used to think that the most important room was the bedroom, but opening night at the Copa taught me that the most important room was the kitchen.

Si and Rita Rose were established in California and they kept begging us to come out. So, one day, I cleared my schedule, packed the car and Anne and I started out on our first cross-country trip. It was a fascinating experience. Two kids from New York's East Side were exposed to the magnificence of our country – the forests, the rivers, the canyons and the ever-changing beautiful desert landscape. We did the obligatory tourist things and enjoyed some special VIP trips through the studios.

I saw an ad for Billy Gray's Bandbox that announced that Buddy Hackett, a truly funny man who was slated to become one of the great stand-up comics, was appearing there nightly. When the show began, someone tapped my shoulder and a voice asked: 'Are you Mickey Freeman?' When I nodded the voice said: 'I'm Sammy Lewis, the owner of the club. Follow me.' I thought I was going to be thrown out for under-age drinking.

When we were in his office he told me that Buddy Hackett had just received an offer to open immediately in Las Vegas and that he needed a replacement. Would I be able to take over for the next ten days? I said: 'I don't even have a tuxedo.' He said: 'This is California. A sports jacket and slacks are considered formal.'

I opened on election night. People don't go out on election night, they stay at home waiting for results. There were three customers in the club and a large TV set centre stage. I wasn't even running and I lost to Eisenhower. However, the rest of the engagement turned out to be successful – both the audience and the critics liked me.

When I got back East, in addition to my regular stand-up comic commitments I also became a specialist – an after dinner speaker for various organisations. When people asked me how I felt about travelling the after-dinner circuit, I said: 'I'd rather follow a good cause than a lousy act.'

Around this time, television opened up for me in the strangest way. Leslie Neilsen and his chanteuse wife, Monica Boyar, were my neighbours in a high-rise apart-ment house. I had worked with Monica and had been instrumental in getting the apartment for them.

One Saturday night, Anne and I attended a party at their home. After a few drinks I started strumming on my ukulele. I admit that my fingering leaves a little to be desired but I play fast and loud and I always dazzle them with my footwork.

On the Monday morning I got a call from Everett Chambers, the casting director for Philco Playhouse, probably the most prestigious dramatic show during the golden days of television. Everett had been at the party and he said: 'This morning when I got to the office there was a script calling for the world's fastest banjo player. That's you. We'll use a banjouke' (a round-shaped ukulele that looked like a banjo). You have the part, 99 per cent.'

'What's the other per cent?'

'We have to check whether you've been a *good* boy.' Suddenly I was exposed to the pressures of the McCarthy era.

I was certified a *good* boy, and found myself doing the most exacting kind of show business – live television! No retakes. No fumbling. No margin for error. All of a sudden I was a real actor, and I went on to many other roles in full hour dramatic productions.

Some time later NBC, not so wisely, broke up one of the great teams of the medium, Sid Caesar and Imogene Coca, and rewarded each of them with their own show.

I was cast as Imogene's boyfriend in a sketch written by Mel Brooks and during the week of rehearsal, Imogene asked if we would mind doing some additional rehearsal at her home. This was a measure of her insecurity. But who could say 'no' to a sweet lady like Imogene?

Imogene lived in a sumptuous brownstone with a winding staircase. It looked the way the home of a star should look. As we ended rehearsal the day before the show, Imogene Coca walked up the winding staircase, looked back over her shoulder and said: 'Maybe I'll die tonight and I won't have to do the show tomorrow.' What a price to pay for success. On show night her live performance, as always, was flawless.

For me, that show was a turning point. It also answered the question I've been asked a thousand times: 'How did you get the part in the *Bilko Show*?' The casting director for CBS saw me on Imogene's show and contacted my agent, Harriet Kaplan. He wanted me to read for a part in a new show starring Phil Silvers. Phil Silvers, Nat Hiken and Kevin Pines, the casting director, auditioned me. I read the opening line of the script for the pilot. The script directions were: soldier in bunk awakened by the sound of the bugle. He says: 'What a wasted night. A hundred million women in America and I had to dream about my brother.' And one of the people in the audition room said: 'He sounds like a real comic.'

Five days later I was in the bathroom showering. Anne yelled in to me: 'CBS called – they want to see you right away.' I jumped into my car and started driving. A few minutes later a cop stopped me – not for speeding but for driving naked.

Working on the *Bilko Show* was marvellous and exciting. And a cheque every week. It was like civil service with make-up.

Whenever we had a hiatus from the *Bilko Show* I would secure a booking on cruise ships to the Caribbean. I had a salary, the sun and Anne all at the same time. What a wonderful deal. My 'two jokes' and my lectures about the *Bilko Show* made me feel like Jules Verne. We got to see places such as Hawaii, Tokyo, Kobe, Hong Kong, Alaska, Mexico, Rio de Janeiro, Montevideo, Chile, Lima, Peru and the Falklands Islands.

In 1987, I was appearing on the SS *Rotterdam's* 103-day world cruise. For my leg of the cruise, Anne and I flew to Rio de Janeiro to board the ship, and from there we sailed for the Falkland Islands and Lima in Peru. Everybody was looking forward to the Falklands. Let's face it, tourists get a little tired of looking at old ruins and old churches, but here was living history. The British had just completed the mop-up of the islands, the troops were still there, the beaches were still mined and we were the first cruise ship to visit the Falklands.

The ship carried about 850 people and about 300 of us were tendered on to the island. A sudden windstorm came up, and in less than an hour it became a point 9 gale. We were taken to a military installation where a Colonel from the Scottish Brigade announced: 'Ladies and gentlemen, because of the storm your ship has put out to sea. You are now under the jurisdiction of the British Army. You will be billeted here for the night. There is tea and soup available. I will see you later at the barracks.' It was a tense moment. Three hundred people saw their luxury cruise turn into a disaster. It was really close to panic. I said to Anne: 'What they need here is a social director.'

I jumped up and announced: 'Attention, ladies and gentlemen! Look at the brighter side of this picture. Do you realise that at this moment we have been in the Falklands longer than the Argentineans? And, let me tell you, war is hell, but the soup is worse. We may be in a gale, but this is one of the only places in the world where you are safe . . . from Amway salesmen.' That broke up the crowd. They applauded, they laughed, they relaxed – and what could have been a terrible disaster turned into a great adventure. I clowned for about 90 minutes. I could almost see the headline in *Variety*: 'Freeman Fractures Them In Falklands.'

I must say that the Holland–American Line was most appreciative of my efforts. Every night when we returned to our cabin, there was a mint on the pillow, but the first night after we had returned to the ship there, on my pillow, were two mints.

One summer I was offered a contract for four back-to-back two-week cruises on the Royal Cruise Line's *Golden Odyssey* sailing out of Athens. What ports of call: Lisbon, Palmas de Majorca, Nice, Mykonos and other Greek Islands. The next summer we did a similar stint on the *Royal Odyssey*, with ports of call including Venice, Dubrovnik, Istanbul, Odessa, Yalta and all of Scandinavia. On those cruises we visited Europe from London to St Petersburg.

One cruise took us to the South Atlantic where we crossed from Dakarta to Barbados. The weather was fine when we left, but after two or three hours a strange haze covered the sun and an announcement came from the bridge: 'Passengers are prohibited from going out on deck.' We were in the middle of a desert sandstorm blowing red sand 200 miles from shore. The sand covered every inch of the ship. It was very startling to be in the middle of a sandstorm that far from land. The captain later explained that this kind of storm was called 'Khamsin', an Arabic word, and in twenty years or so he had seen this phenomenon only two or three times.

On another cruise, we had just left the island of Mykonos and were enjoying a midnight snack when a Greek announcement came over the PA system – short, cryptic, tense. I said to Anne: 'That's unusual. The PA system is generally not used at this hour.' Three minutes later came another Greek announcement, even more excited. Officers began disappearing from the dining room. A few minutes later the cruise director, trying to look casual, passed my table. I asked him what was happening and he said: 'Nothing that you should worry about.'

This was my cue to go out on deck and look over the side of the ship to see what was going on. It was a spectacle I'll never forget – flames shooting out of the side of the ship. The smoke got into the ventilating system and passengers who had gone to bed early woke to find themselves in haze-filled cabins. People ran up on deck in pyjamas and bathrobes. Yet normal shipboard life was going full blast – the bars were open and the disco was functioning. I suggested to Anne that we go to the disco and dance. I figured that would help calm the crowd because if we were dancing the situation could not be very serious. As we danced, people kept running between us with suitcases and lifejackets, some even with blankets and bottles of water. Anne said: 'I think it's not working.' I went out on the deck again to see what was happening. The captain had steered the ship so we were in sight of the shore. The fire was coming out of the laundry and a firewall had been dropped to isolate the flames. Crewmen in asbestos suits had been sent down to extinguish the flames and as I watched the fire came under control. This was a happy ending to a potential disaster.

The next night, before my show, the captain asked me to make light of the fire. I opened the show with this line: 'Who was the wise guy who ordered his laundry well done?'

Some years later we were out to dinner with Larry and Pat Gelbart. (Larry Gelbart is the creator and writer of the television series *M*A*S*H*, the writer of *Tootsie, Oh God!*, the Broadway smashes *A Funny Thing Happened On The Way To The Forum, The City Of Angels* and many more.)

The next morning Larry called me. 'Mickey, you know your face got stuck in my head.' I said: 'I thought it was heartburn.' Larry continued: 'I'm doing a play right now called *One Two Three Four Five*. It's a biblical musical and there is a part in there that would be perfect for you.' I said: 'When is it happening?' Larry said: 'Right now.' 'Now is impossible, I'm very busy on the after-dinner circuit. In fact, tonight I have four hundred Catholics with fruit cups waiting for me in Cleveland.' 'I'm here on Fifth Avenue. Come up to the apartment and read the play.' Who was I to turn down a Larry Gelbart play?

After I read the script I realised it was a cameo role. Larry thought I could play an ancient sage. There were five continuous pages of monologue. I said: 'Larry, you expect me to memorise all of this?' Larry looked at me, hurt: 'Would I write a concerto that no one could play?' Gelbart's confidence won me over and I agreed to take the part.

After a few days of rehearsal I was told to report to make-up. The make-up man held different beards to my face and when he was satisfied, he pasted the foliage on me – a combination of Santa Claus and Abraham

Lincoln. Gelbart came in to check out the finished product, and said: 'Take that beard off and give me back the real Mickey Freeman.' I have to admit that it was somewhat disconcerting to play an old sage without make-up.

This was the first time I appeared on stage in a real play. To a couple of the drama columnists who interviewed me, I said: 'I'm glad to be in *One Two Three Four Five*. I finally got in to a show that counts.' Of all the shows that Gelbart had written, this was the only one that didn't make Broadway.

My next stage appearance was on Broadway at the Helen Hayes Theatre. I had been offered the part of a taxi driver in a show called *Three From Brooklyn*. I read some of the dialogue and walked away from the part. When the show opened a capable actor, Ray Serra, played the taxi driver who described the wonders of Brooklyn and also served as MC and introduced the various performers. The critics hated the show and I said: 'God was good to me. I'm not in this one.' The show opened on a Friday night and the following Sunday morning at 7 a.m. I got a call from the stage manager of the show. She told me that Ray Serra had called in with a serious throat condition and his doctor felt that he couldn't perform for a long time. Would I come to the theatre, she pleaded, as a favour to Sal Richards, the star of the show and a brother Friar. The ailing Serra, she continued, was also a brother Friar. My professional credo has always been that the show must go on. But why was I chosen to keep it on?

I got to the theatre at 11 a.m. and the stage manager handed me the script. I said: 'How long before you expect me to do this?' She said: 'Four hours. You're on at the three o'clock matinee.' I've always been a quick learner, but this was ridiculous. Then suddenly I realised

I was playing a cab driver and it was logical for me to carry a clipboard. What better place to write down the cues? I turned to the producer and said: 'I will play the part on one condition. The lines I speak will be my own. I'm sure you know what the critics had to say about your lines.' At this point he was ready to say yes to anything. The show was beyond redemption, but I feel that my taxi driver and my improvised lines were certainly a great improvement.

In New York there is a magnificent building housing the Museum of Broadcasting. I got a call from Ron Simon, the curator of the museum, who told me that they would like to do an evening dedicated to the *Bilko Show*. They were planning to show a *Bilko* episode in which I appeared, followed by my lecture about the show and the people who were in it.

After the lecture was announced, the response was terrific, and the museum had to change the locale from a lecture room to a theatre. A lot of people wanted to hear me talk about a forty-year-old television show. I asked the audience: 'Does anyone here feel that the show is dated?' They all called out 'No, no, no'. And that was the secret of the show – no jokes, no one-liners, but situations and characters that stay funny forever.

I have been a member of the New York Friars Club for many years. Every time I enter the English Renaissance Building known as The Monastery I get a satisfying sense of being surrounded by great talent – performing talent, writing talent, musical talent, producing talent – the creative people who are today's headliners and stars, as well as the original, creative performers and writers who have graced the building for a century. George M. Cohan said it best long ago. 'The Friars Club is dedicated to Art, Literature and Good Fellowship.' Frank Sinatra was the Abbot of the Friars for many years, and other

Abbots included George M. Cohan, Milton Berle and Alan King. I go to the Friars to enjoy the cuisine, trade witticisms with fellow members, catch up on the latest trade news, but most of all I go to the Friars to savour the contentment of being part of American show business.

The New York Friars Club is a fraternal organisation and the Friars Foundation raises hundreds of thousands of dollars each year. This money is shared out to performing arts institutions and colleges.

The tradition of entertaining the entertainers goes back many decades. Each year sees a Friar Frolic. Irving Berlin wrote *Alexander's Ragtime Band* for the first Friar Frolic in 1911. The Annual Frolics were galas written and performed by the best of the era. Some years ago the Frolics were replaced by the Annual Testimonial Dinners and Celebrity Roasts – the Roast is the flip side of a Testimonial.

At a Celebrity Roast some of the keenest creative minds shoot their sharpest barbs at a Guest of Honour, a major show-business celebrity who is pleased and proud to be insulted by his peers. For example, at a Roast for Henny Youngman, I said: 'He is the king of the one-liners because he can't remember two.' When we roasted Sid Caesar, I said: 'Sid, don't stay up north, go to Florida. There you can be a sex symbol – you look like every widow's late husband.'

For me, the Caesar Roast was one of special nights of my career. It was a sell-out affair in one of the major gambling casinos in Atlantic City. At dinner that night, Sid related a fascinating story. Sid has always been intrigued by physics. One day when he was rehearsing *Show of Shows* his secretary told him that there was a call from Professor Albert Einstein. Sid turned to his writers and said: 'We have two days left to show time. There's no time left for practical jokes.' The secretary said: 'This is no joke, Professor Einstein's office is on the phone.' When Sid got on the phone, Einstein's secretary said that the professor asked if Sid could meet with the famous scientist on Monday in Princeton, New Jersey, where Einstein lived.

Sid hung up the phone and told his secretary to go out and buy all the books on relativity that she could find. I said: 'You were planning to learn about relativity over the weekend?' Sid replied: 'I wanted to know something about it. I could hardly wait for Sunday to pass. On Monday, when I turned on the TV, there was the flash – Professor Einstein had been found dead in Princeton.' Sid continued: 'It was a great frustration that I never got to meet the professor. About a year later I was giving a pseudo lecture in Washington, DC, to a group of diplomats and scientists. After my lecture I was approached by a man who introduced himself as Professor Robert Oppenheimer, who had been one of the scientists who had worked on the atom bomb and was close to Einstein. Oppenheimer complimented me on my performance and said: 'I'm sorry that my good friend Albert Einstein was not here today to hear you. You were his favourite performer.' Sid said to us: 'That is the magic of television. That people of such stature would invite me into their home.'

Sid was right. One of the fringe benefits of show business is that thousands, millions, of people let you come into their hearts and lives. Next to my relationship with my high school sweetheart, Anne, who became my wife, was the relationship I had with the *Bilko Show* – Nat Hiken, the platoon and, especially, Phil Silvers.

Working with Phil Silvers was rewarding, but I regret that he did very little socialising with the people on the show. One of the reasons was that he was hardly finished with one episode when he had to start memorising the script for the next. He was always concerned about lines – his lines for the show, the morning line at the race track, and the telephone line to his bookmaker. Phil once said about the *Bilko* platoon: 'We were a remarkable family. There was never really a harsh word or an incident of even semi-major consequence'. That probably was one of reasons we were such a success.

Every day in show business is like going to school. In my almost fifty years as a performer I've learned a great deal from the people I worked with. Working with Phil was a scholarship to the world of timing, takes and taste. Being with Phil, week in, week out, was the equivalent of a PhD in 'funny'. It made the rest of my professional life easy.

11 The Cast and Crew

SOME WELL-KNOWN NAMES WHO APPEARED IN THE
SERIES

Alan Alda	TV and film star
Lucille Ball*	Major film and TV star
Red Barber	Sports announcer
Orson Bean	Comic/actor
Yogi Berra	Baseball player
Sammy Cahn	Songwriter
Peggy Cass	Actor
Dick Cavett	TV star
Irwin Corey	Comedy professor
Bing Crosby	Major film and TV star
Dagmar	TV star
Bill Dana	TV star
Whitey Ford	Baseball player
Tony Galento	Boxer
Dody Goodman	TV star
Pat Hingle	Stage and film actor
Jane Kean	Actress/singer
George Kennedy	Actor
Kay Kendall	Film star

* The great Lucy appeared briefly in an episode called 'Bilko's Ape Man'.
There was no screen credit for her performance.

Dean Martin	Major film and TV star
Gil McDougal	Baseball player
McGuire Sisters	Singing trio
Kay Medford	Stage and screen actor
Dina Merrill	Film actor
Carlos Montalban	Actor
Robert Morse	Actor
Tom Poston	TV actor
Phil Rizzuto	Baseball player
Mickey Rooney	Film star
Sam Snead	Golfer
Jule Styne	Composer
Ed Sullivan	TV host
Mike Todd	Producer for stage and film
Dan Topping	Owner of the New York Yankees
Dick Van Dyke	Major TV star
Ziggy the Chimp	Primate

THE REGULARS . . . AND THE IRREGULARS

Phil Silvers	Master Sgt Ernie Bilko
Harvey Lembeck	Cpl Rocco Barbella
Herbie Faye	Pvt Sam Fender
Paul Ford	Col John Hall
Maurice Gosfield	Pvt Duane Doberman
Joe E. Ross	Sgt Rupert Ritzik
Allan Melvin	Cpl Henshaw
Billy Sands	Pvt Dino Paparelli
Mickey Freeman	Pvt Fielding Zimmerman
Hope Sansberry	Nell Hall
Jimmy Little	Sgt Grover
Harry Clark	Sgt Sowici
Ned Glass	Sgt Pendelton
Karl Lukas	Pvt Kadowski
P. Jay Sidney	Pvt Palmer

Jack Healy	Pvt Mullen
Bernie Fein	Pvt Gomez
Walter Cartier	Pvt Dillingham
Jim Perry	Lt Anderson
Tige Andrews	Pvt Gander
Maurice Brenner	Pvt Fleischman
Terry Carter	Pvt Sugarman
John Gibson	Chaplain
Elisabeth Fraser	Sgt Joan Hogan

THE PEOPLE WITHOUT WHOM A TV SHOW CAN'T WORK

SEASON ONE:

Produced and staged by Nat Hiken
Directed by Al De Caprio
Photographed by William J. Miller
Supervised by Edward J. Montagne
Editors: Sy Singer, Ray Sandiford
Art directors: Don Gilman, Al Brenner
Production manager: M. Clay Adams
Music: John Strauss
Additional music: Hank Sylvern
Recording engineer: James Shields
Assistant to producer: Kevin Pines
Settings: Jack Landau
Filmed by Kenco Films Inc.

Writers: Arnold Auerbach, Barry Blitzer, Vincent Bogart, Nat Hiken, Coleman Jacoby, Harvey Orkin, Arnie Rosen, Terry Ryan, Tony Webster

SEASON TWO:

As above, except:
Editor: Ray Sandiford

Art director: Richard Jackson
Additional art direction: Robert Rowe Paddock
Additional staging: Charles Friedman

New writers: Billy Friedberg, Leonard Stern, Aaron
Ruben, Phil Sharp, Lou Meltzer, Sydney Zelinka

SEASON THREE:

As above, except:
Staged by Aaron Ruben
New writers: A.J. Russell, Neil Simon, Paul Jordan

SEASON FOUR:

As above, except:
Produced by: Edward J. Montagne

Episode Guide

Season One 1955/1956
(Dates indicate first US broadcast)

1. NEW RECRUITS 20/9/55
Bilko has just lost $250 of other people's money in a poker game with the master sergeants. The chaplain points out that a mirror has been moved in Bilko's room giving the other players a clear view of Bilko's cards. The loss of the money hurts, but losing to chicanery really is a blow to Bilko's pride. New recruits are smartly marched in by Private Higgins. Bilko gives his standard welcoming speech and starts to hustle the youngsters for whatever money they have brought from home. He is stymied at every suggestion by Higgins, a military school graduate, who knows every comma of the rule-book. After taps, Higgins asks Bilko to take care of $320 of the men's money. The chaplain has said that Sergeant Slick-Operator is trustworthy. Despite the chaplain's opinion, Bilko doesn't trust himself. He puts the money under Higgins' pillow and Henshaw and Rocco, holding rifles, guard it all night.

2. EMPTY STORE 27/9/55
Sergeants Pendelton, Grover and Sowici clobbered Bilko at poker. The trio has also cleaned out a new recruit

holding his buddies' cash. This is against Bilko's ethics – new recruits are not fair game for seasoned army gamblers. Bilko instructs Rocco to rent an empty store in town. Word of the deal spreads through the camp. The sergeants are sure that Bilko is on to something really big; they want in. They try to soften Sergeant Smooth-Operator up: the quartermaster sergeant brings Bilko a newly issued jacket; the electrical sergeant installs a private telephone in Bilko's room; the mess sergeant brings special foods and all kinds of goodies. Showing great reluctance, Bilko rents each of them a third of the store, cash in advance. The renters want to know what kind of business Bilko is planning. Bilko explains that they each have a third of an empty store – there is no business. Bilko returns the cash to the new recruits but he doesn't recoup his own losses because Rocco has leased six more empty stores.

3. WAC 4/10/55

Bilko, a great reader of the small type in Army orders, discovers that a personal jeep goes to the master sergeant who volunteers to check the armoury doors every day. He has to be very careful about this. If the other sergeants see his name posted as a volunteer, they, too, will volunteer – they are aware that Bilko knows every regulation inside and out. He convinces them that they don't want the job. A new master sergeant, J. Hogan, also volunteers for the job. Turns out *she* also reads fine print and she, too, wants the personal jeep. Joan knows all about Bilko and his fancy ways. Joan is blonde, beautiful, blue eyed and smart. She is filled with as much guile as Bilko. It's up to the colonel to decide who gets the jeep. The finagler tries to swamp her with paperwork so she won't have time to volunteer; J. Hogan counters his every move. Bilko tries to romance her; she doesn't buy it. She bats her eyes at him and he falls for her.

4. THE HORSE 11/10/55

Bilko uses platoon money to buy a racehorse with a bad leg. He hopes to get the leg cured and race the horse at the big tracks. The horse is hidden in an old gunnery shed. One of the platoon members who has worked with horses tells Bilko that the animal has a bowed tendon. He will never be able to race. A general is coming to inspect Fort Baxter. Universal consternation from the colonel down. Colonel Hall is doing his own pre-inspection inspection. The equine platoon member is moved to the guesthouse. The general arrives at the guesthouse. When he sees the horse he embraces Colonel Hall and thanks him for going to the trouble of putting a horse in his quarters. They both served in the cavalry before the army was mechanised and he is touched by this thoughtful gesture. Bilko wonders if the general would like to buy the horse.

5. A.W.O.L. 18/10/55

Steve Nagy, the motor pool's carburettor expert always goes A.W.O.L. when his Hungarian family has problems. He has just gone A.W.O.L. again. Without him, the ailing trucks and jeeps pile up. Bilko is ordered to bring the errant carburettor guru back from Chicago in a hurry. Bilko arrives at Steve's home where a party is going on to celebrate the engagement of his sister, Magda. Steve has just negotiated a settlement between the two families over Magda's dowry. There's czardas dancing, drinking and Hungarian card games. Bilko is drawn into the card game, which he does not even begin to understand. He keeps winning. The groom's father accuses Bilko of being a cardsharp brought in by the bride's family to

'The Horse'

recover the dowry money that they have paid over. The wedding is off. Bilko tries to repair the damage he has unwittingly done and finally gets Steve's sister and her intended together again.

6. BOXER 25/10/55

Dino Paparelli is training for the inter-platoon boxing tournament. Dino knows the standard moves that fighters use but, when *he* performs them, it looks more like ballet than boxing. Paparelli has courage – what he lacks are muscles. The mess sergeant has had Cpl Eagan transferred to his kitchen. The corporal knows nothing about cooking, but he's good at clobbering an opponent. Handsome Claude Dillingham comes by to check with Bilko about his garden. Claude was an amateur boxing champ. He gives Paparelli pugilistic advice. Bilko bets a hundred dollars that Dillingham will beat Eagan. But Dillingham's fiancée (who packs a mean punch herself) has forbidden him to fight. Dillingham only blows his cool if someone disparages flowers. Bilko incites Eagen to hate chrysanthemums. Eagan taunts Dillingham about his favourite bloom and the two GIs are about to have at each other. The chaplain intervenes. The two fighters refuse to fight. They're planning to garden together.

7. THE HOODLUM 1/11/55

Bilko is bucking for 'Soldier of the Month'. Ernie is not inspired by the honour as much as by the three-day pass that goes with it. The colonel is struggling with Pvt Parker, who is working on a dishonourable discharge. The hoodlum is sent to the motor pool. Maybe Bilko can straighten him out. Bilko, Rocco and Henshaw scam the tough GI into believing that they are going to liberate the gold in Fort Knox using tanks and explosives. Parker is inducted into the operation, and is told that once in, there is no way out. Parker is assigned all sorts of tasks that he is assured are important to the heist: unloading cans of food for the mess; outfitting new recruits for the quartermaster; standing guard duty all night. The colonel is impressed with the change in the young man. Parker comes to Bilko and pleads to be let out of the Fort Knox heist. Bilko releases him, on condition that Parker will be an obedient soldier. Bilko does not get the 'Soldier of the Month' award, Parker does.

8. MARDI GRAS (a.k.a. THE MOTOR POOL MARDI GRAS) 8/11/55

The motor pool is converting a jeep into a float for Rosedale's annual Mardi Gras. By lot, Doberman has been chosen King of the Mardi Gras. It's the king's privilege to choose his queen. Doberman has a crush on Joy Landers, a local young socialite. Some of the platoon go to her house and offer her the 'queenship'. She turns the offer down and laughs at the men. Bilko is offended and determines to punish her. He diddles her into believing that Doberman is magnificent, romantic, desirable. When Joy finally meets him, he tells her to 'Get lost'. She throws herself at Duane's feet and begs. Everyone laughs at her. The next day she turns up at the platoon and apologises. She had been mocking people all her life and finally she has found out how it feels to be laughed at. In apology, she takes over the decoration of the motor pool float.

9. THE EATING CONTEST (a.k.a. THE STOMACH) 15/11/55

Pvt Honnergar (Fred Gwynne) joins company B. Some of the men recognise him – he was the eating champion of the army. Company A has a favourite trencherman

'The Eating Contest'

too. Bilko challenges Company A, and puts his money where Honnergar's stomach is. Bilko has a test run, but the champ eats only a mouthful of steak before he is full. Bilko does some detective work and finds out that 'The Stomach' only eats gluttonously when he is miserable. He was in love with a girl who sent him a 'Dear John' letter and was a great eater as long as he continued to mourn. Bilko plays records that make Ed sad, weeps with Ed over his lost love, gives him anti-pep talks. The desolate 'stomach' is all appetite. The eat-off is at a local hotel and Ed eats his opponent under the table.

10. THE CENTENNIAL 22/11/55
Special Service Lieutenant Parker descends on Fort Baxter. His ambition: to be a captain. His method: to root out all gambling and bring art and culture to Fort Baxter. Bilko is his assistant. Bilko mentions that the hundredth anniversary of Fort Baxter will soon occur. He suggests a Centennial Celebration. Bilko has a small book of the history of the fort and is assigned to write and direct the pageant. Parker gets to see Bilko's work. The founder of Fort Baxter was a scoundrel who sold the local Indians whiskey. Bilko is ordered to rewrite. The centennial is now 75 years of Fort Baxter. During the Civil War, Colonel 'Honest John' Otis had his closest friend shot on the flimsiest evidence. Parker reschedules. The pageant is down to 50 years of Fort Baxter. During the Spanish–American war the commanding officer of Fort Baxter sold out the secrets of the army for a few moments with the glamorous spy, Mata Lopez. Parker cancels all celebrations. He forgets culture and joins in Bilko's regular poker game.

11. BIVOUAC 29/11/55

Once a year, all the men at Fort Baxter bivouac in the woods for a week to hone their camping skills and tone their muscles. All the men, that is, except Bilko and three other master sergeants, who somehow land in the hospital isolation ward with mysterious maladies, whose symptoms are brilliantly recreated by the acting abilities of Bilko. They regain their health through a strict regimen of dancing with the nurses, drinking champagne, and playing poker. The colonel is aware of Bilko's charade but the flimflammer always takes in the medical officers. This year, the colonel is determined that Bilko *will* go on bivouac. A new medical officer tries to outscam Bilko by convincing the great faker that he really has a fatal disease. Bilko takes to his bed, the nurses weep, the colonel brings flowers and consolation. When the medical trickery is revealed the colonel orders Bilko out of bed and into the field with his men. A beaten Bilko sadly leaves the isolation ward, but on the way out, he falls and sprains his ankle and has to spend a week in bed.

12. THE SINGING CONTEST 06/12/55

The platoon has only one ambition in the world: to get warm. The furnace in the barracks is broken and the potbellied stove is no defence against the Kansas cold. The army has announced a Glee Club contest, which will be held on the outskirts of Miami, which is in 90-degree heat. Bilko tries to whip his platoon of monotones into a musical organisation. His soloist is Doberman, whose voice is worse than his looks. Bilko bets *against* his own men, using the platoon's welfare fund. Even Bilko admits that it's a disloyal act – but money is money. Rookie Pvt Breaker proves to be a wonderful tenor. To save his bet, Bilko tries to get rid of Breaker,

'Singing Contest'

using typical hustler scams. At the last moment he changes his mind, and sells his car to cover his bet. The men get their money and win their way to Florida. The softhearted con man is stuck in the cold of Fort Baxter on special assignment.

13. THE TWITCH (a.k.a. THE LECTURE) 13/12/55

Colonel Hall complains to Captain Whitney about the incessant gambling in the camp, all of it controlled by Sergeant Bilko. Captain Whitney suggests that the men need cultural activities. He mentions that his wife, Gloria, delivers an inspiring lecture about Beethoven that she has performed at other forts. The colonel orders Bilko to arrange the lecture. One of the men has heard Gloria in Manila. He reports that she tugs at her girdle as she speaks (this was in an era when women still wore girdles). She has earned the nickname of *the twitch* because of this habit. Bilko organises a pool – the winner being the man who predicts how many tugs she will make during her speech. On the night of the event, the recreation hall is packed, other camps are networked to Baxter via short-wave radio. As the lecturer talks, she tugs, and the men chant in unison 'twenty-two, twenty-three'. With Gloria's final word the chant is 'twenty-five'. Cheers and applause.

14. REUNION 20/12/55

The wartime squad, which Bilko had led through dangerous battles in the Pacific, is having a tenth-anniversary reunion in New York. The group has great affection and respect for Bilko. He is sure they will be impressed that he is now a master sergeant. He checks into a suite in the Waldorf Astoria and is in a robe when he meets his old buddies. They are all much more prosperous than he is. Bilko is awed and embarrassed by their financial standings. As he is dressing for dinner in a *rented* tuxedo, he realises that his sergeant's uniform is nothing to be ashamed of. When he walks into the dining room, his old buddies are all as impressed with him as he had hoped they'd be. One of his ex-platoon mates offers him a job in New York. Bilko declines and returns to Fort Baxter, a happy man.

15. RICH KID 27/12/55

A replacement recruit, Tommy Thompson, reports to Bilko. An officer ushers in a reporter who pretends that he is doing a story on new trainees. He pulls out a clipping of Thompson in formal dress. Thompson is the heir to two-hundred million dollars. The headline proclaims that the rich young man has disappeared. Tommy pleads with the reporter to keep his secret and give him a chance to see if he can be accepted for himself. The reporter agrees. Bilko overhears and orders the platoon to treat Tommy as an ordinary soldier. They go to a café that Bilko wants to buy. Tommy gives Bilko a signed cheque and tells him to fill it in for any amount. Bilko is tempted to write a big check. But he can't do it. He enters only the amount the platoon has laid out for Tommy. Tommy admits that he has used up his immediate funds and he won't get his inheritance for another ten years.

16. HOLLYWOOD 3/1/56

A Hollywood studio is making a picture about the battle of Kabuchi. The studio PR department has called the Pentagon to find a GI who fought in that battle and is still in service. The army comes up with Bilko. He is assigned to be technical adviser. The studio wants Bilko to meet with the press and state that the film will be accurate – and then go home. Bilko makes the required statement.

Sergeant Brass-Nerve bullies and blackmails the producers to let him come on the set. As a sop to his vanity they insert a tiny part in which an actor called 'Bilko' passes the ammunition. Bilko is not satisfied with the actor chosen to portray him. Sixty-five people are auditioned for the part and Bilko is still not appeased. In desperation the head of the studio closes down the production.

17. INVESTIGATION (a.k.a. THE BIG INVESTIGATION) 10/1/56

Bilko is alerted that a congressional committee is on its way to Fort Baxter. They're coming to check on rumoured waste in the military and 'country-club' living by the enlisted personnel. There are threats of budget and salary cuts. Not since Valley Forge have American soldiers lived in the kind of poverty that Bilko shows the committee. The impression is created that the platoon goes barefoot; sleeps on boards; shares a single hot dog for their meal; they even get food packages from Poland. Bilko stage-manages the post activities so that the colonel's wife appears to be taking in laundry. The committee is so distressed that they promise the platoon that they will get them $10-a-week rises. When the colonel discovers Bilko's tricks he takes the committee back to the barracks where they find the 'impoverished' platoon drinking beer, eating turkey and swilling champagne.

18. KIDS IN TRAILER 17/1/56

Pvt O'Brien's wife and three small children have driven in a trailer to Fort Baxter. Bilko drives O'Brien to the trailer and is touched by the family. He sends the private and his wife off for three days alone. A WAC takes care of the two cute kids and their infant sibling until the WAC gets sudden orders and must leave immediately. No

'Kids in Trailer'

other woman on the post is available. Bilko baby-sits – diaper changing included. Bilko can't cope alone and sneaks the kids back to barracks. The five-year-old boy knows every regulation in the army book and is disappointed by the appearance of the barracks and its inhabitants. The platoon is abashed and cleans up everything in sight, including themselves. The boy is satisfied that his father was right – Company B is the best platoon in the army. The by-the-book youngster reports to Colonel Hall that his dad is A.W.O.L. The colonel gets the whole story and congratulates Company B. Mrs Hall takes care of the children.

19. REVOLUTIONARY WAR 24/1/56
Bilko's Aunt Minerva sends him a box containing mementos of his great, great, grand-uncle, Joshua Bilko, a major on George Washington's staff. In the box are a broken sword, a diary and a medal inscribed: 'To Joshua Bilko, presented for help rendered our nation'. Bilko experiences pride of family. He applies for Officer's Training School. He reads aloud from Uncle Bilko's diary (which is re-enacted). Uncle Josh flirts with Martha Washington, gambles, runs a turkey raffle (which he wins) and eats a turkey leg in front of the starving men. Washington had broken the sword when Uncle Bilko failed to show up for a battle. And finally, when Washington is about to cross the Delaware, Bilko sells seats in the boats. All space is sold out when Washington boards and the supreme general is forced to stand. The medal praising his service to the nation is from the British. When Bilko finishes reading, he has Henshaw bury the mementos as deeply as possible.

20. TRANSFER 31/1/56

Colonel Hall has just returned from Washington. His staff car is not at the station. The colonel is angry. He hitches a ride on the back of a motorcycle. His staff car passes him at eighty miles an hour – Bilko is driving, one hand on the steering wheel, the other arm around a platinum blonde. The colonel is furious. Back at his office he discovers Bilko has pulled off other scams, and he goes ballistic. Bilko is equally angry and applies for a transfer, which the Colonel gladly grants. The colonel at the new post is an easy-going officer who not only tolerates Bilko's scams he is amused by them. Colonel Hall is unhappy. Bilko's replacement drives him crazy with efficiency and promptness. He berates his staff – something he has never done before. He yearns for Bilko. At the same time, Bilko is equally unhappy. The sergeants at his new post are too easy to beat at cards; the enlisted men are too eager to hand him money for his schemes. He likes his suckers to put up a fight. He yearns for Fort Baxter.

21. THE REST CURE 7/2/56

Fort Baxter is sweating out a heat wave that would do the tropics proud. The platoon watches a newsreel that describes Camp Paradise, high in the Rocky Mountains, where fatigued army personnel, who show psychiatric symptoms are sent to recover. It's cool and beautiful. There are pools and tennis courts and even skiing and ice-skating. Bilko changes the personnel reports that go to the Pentagon to include a 'Private Marilyn Monroe' and submits a transportation equipment inventory that shows that, in addition to motorised vehicles, the platoon has six oxen and a yak. When Major Friend at the Pentagon reads these indications of mental disturbances, he hurries out to Fort Baxter. As soon as Bilko hears of his pending arrival, he starts training his people in 'real crazy'. The major is soon convinced that he has an entire platoon of disturbed soldiers that must be sent to Camp Paradise. The colonel realises the scam.

22. DINNER AT SOWICI'S 14/2/56
Master Sergeants Joan Hogan and Ernie Bilko attend the wedding of a GI couple. Weddings always hit Bilko hard. During the ceremony Joan holds his arm tightly and puts her blonde head on his shoulder. Thinking to show Joan how bad marriage can be, he visits Sergeant Sowici's home. The apartment is a disaster; Emma Sowici is frumpy and family discourse is vociferous and nasty. Bilko invites himself and Joan to dinner. Emma and her husband are so touched that anyone would want to have dinner in their home that love blooms again. When Ernie and Joan arrive, the house is spotless, Emma beautifully dressed, dinner wonderful, host and hostess much in love. After dinner, Emma is upset because Bilko wastes his nights playing poker with no loving home to come too. Joan leaves in tears. When Bilko finds her, she apologises for breaking down and says that she does not want to get married – she has her career etc. Bilko is left pleading and confused.

23. ARMY MEMOIRS 21/2/56
Colonel Hall lambastes Sergeants Pendelton, Sowicki and Grover for their poor performance ratings. The only sergeant with a perfect record is Bilko (he never sends in reports). The trembling trio claim that Bilko caused their deficiencies. Bilko altered a quartermaster requisition and ordered air-force jackets with mouton collars, all in his size. The electrical sergeant blames Bilko for having him install a direct telephone line to a betting parlour; the mess sergeant blames Bilko for his negative sanitary

report – Bilko had solicited bets on cockroach races in the kitchen. The colonel reduces Bilko to private. Bilko vows to have his stripes back within twelve hours. The Scheming Sergeant requisitions a typewriter. Shortly, the gossip is that Bilko is writing a book that will expose scandals at Fort Baxter. Bilko really knows nothing but, in his clever conversations with the 'snitching sergeants', suggests that he knows a great deal about past peccadillos. By the end of the day the 'tattling three' beg the colonel to restore Bilko's stripes.

24. MISS AMERICA 28/2/56

Bilko chastises his men for not participating in the 'Sweetheart of the Platoon Contest'. Entry fee: a mere $10 to defray the cost of thumb tacks. Only one man has submitted a picture of his girlfriend to be pinned to the bulletin board. Shy Pvt Honnergar submits a picture of his sweetheart, Peggy. The platoon and Bilko are blown away by Peggy's looks. She's the most beautiful woman any of them have ever seen. That face could make Bilko a millionaire. Sergeant-Con starts the publicity campaign and gets Peggy invited to the Topeka finals for Miss Kansas. When he finally meets Peggy, she is indeed a beautiful woman – of sixty. Honergar's sweetheart is his mother and the picture he submitted was forty years old. Peggy has travelled with her own apron and rolling pin. When she heard the word 'contest' she thought that she was participating in a 'bake-off'.

25. THE COURT MARTIAL 6/3/56

The army has asked Colonel Hall, CO of Fort Baxter, to process 309 new recruits in three hours. A general is at the Fort to observe. A new inductee, Chapman, comes in with a chimpanzee. The chimp, Chapman and his

'The Court Martial'

Bilko can't fool Sgt Hogan, but the Colonel is falling for his double
talk as usual. Phil Silvers with Elizabeth Fraser and Paul Ford.

Left Bilko persuades Zimmerman to date Doberman's sister using a double bluff that ultimately back-fires on him.

Below Following the dream sequence, Bilko muscles in on Zimmerman's date with Doberman's sister – but Bilko's dream date turns into his worst nightmare.

Above Mickey Freeman as Private Zimmerman.

Above See no evil, hear no evil, speak no evil – in 'The Court Martial', a chimp stood trial. Nick Saunders played Captain Barker and Barbara Barry was WAC Edna.

Top right deep concentration from the cast as Aaron Reuben directs a scene.

Bottom right The platoon on parade during their first appearance on the *Ed Sullivan Show*.

Below Director Nat Hiken rehearses a scene with Phil Silvers, Allan Melvin (Henshaw) and Harvey Lembeck (Rocco).

Above Zimmerman (Mickey Freeman) and Paparelli (Billy Sands) service the US Army's cleanest jeep in Bilko's motor pool.

Maurice Gosfield (Doberman) shows off his impressive physique to
Harvey Lembeck (Rocco), Allan Melvin (Henshaw) and Phil Silvers.

brother are a stage act. The brother is late and Chapman does not want to leave his hairy partner alone. He takes the chimp with him. When the chimp is asked his name, he chatters and the officer says, 'Hurry, speak up'. The non-com, without looking up, writes his name as Harry Speak Up. In their hurry, no one looks at the inductees. When the general realizes what has happened, he acts quickly to save himself from being laughed out of the service. The chimp is court-martialled, Bilko is his defence attorney and the charge is biting the company cook. Bilko's claims the chimp thought the cook's thick fingers were bananas. Chapman testifies that the only way his family can make a living is because of the talents of the chimp. The chimp is released as a hardship case.

26. FURLOUGH IN NEW YORK 13/3/56

Sgt Joan Hogan is on furlough in New York City to renew friendships with men she dated. Sgt Ernie Bilko is on furlough in New York City to renew friendships with women he dated. Both arrive at Grand Central Terminal. They phone around. No one is available. Bored and lonely they head for the YM/YWCA for showers, steam room and a nap. Ernie does not realise that he has gone to the YWCA by mistake. He showers, takes steam and heads for a nap. He ends up in the same room as Joan. She is already tucked in the lower bunk. Ernie takes the upper bunk. His snoring drives Joan out. Back at Fort Baxter. Joan is doing paper work and asks Ernie for his serial number. He looks at his dog tags. He is wearing Joan's tags and she is wearing his. The only place they could have taken off their tags is in the steam room at the New York YWCA. They could have spent a week together in New York.

27. THE BIG URANIUM STRIKE 20/3/56

Bilko overhears that there is uranium to be found in Fort Baxter. He is determined to find the radioactive material, get the area condemned, buy it for a few cents an acre and enrich himself by reselling it. Doberman is loaded down with a Geiger counter and searches the Fort. The uranium appears to be in Colonel Hall's basement. Sgt Con Man persuades the colonel and his wife that they have a dinner date with a general in a nearby army installation. The platoon tries to demolish the basement with all kinds of explosive devices. The colonel returns and, when he demands to know what's going on, Bilko explains that the men, because of their love and admiration for the colonel, are converting his basement into a play room. Bilko eventually discovers that, during the war, atomic tests had been conducted in the area and the workers' overalls had been buried in thirty feet of concrete at the spot where the colonel's house now stands.

28. BILKO AND THE BEAST 27/3/56

Colonel Hall assigns a tough drill sergeant to Bilko's platoon. His orders: shape up men who have never drilled in the eight years that Bilko has been in charge. What Sergeant Quentin Benson – a.k.a. The Beast – lacks in brains, he makes up in brutality. His 'secretary', Corporal Krim, announces that The Beast is taking over everything: raffles, gambling, dances and even Bilko's room. Bilko, much to the disgust of the platoon, does not fight back. Bilko persuades the Beast that the men have taken out a $100,000 insurance policy on him because they respect him. The Beast is very proud of being worth $100,000, until Krim explains that The Beast is worth that kind of money only when he is dead. The Beast refuses food prepared by Bilko and panics when he sees

Fleishman sharpening a bayonet. The silent pressure from the platoon gets so great that The Beast and Krim flee camp.

29. THE PHYSICAL CHECKUP (a.k.a. THE PHYSICAL) 10/4/56

A surprise twenty-mile hike is ordered for the platoon. Bilko visits the colonel and pleads a fictitious disease that interferes with his walking. The colonel gives in with hardly any protest and suggests that, at Bilko's age, a long hike could prove to be too much. Bilko complains to Joan that the colonel wants to get rid of him because he has gotten older. Joan explains that the colonel knows that Bilko is the best motor pool sergeant in the army and needs him. A special medical officer will be giving physicals the next day. Bilko determines to exercise all day and night. He works out vigorously (for Bilko). He collapses from all the unaccustomed activity. The examiner is amazed at Ernie's fatigue and criticises the colonel for overworking Bilko. He suggests that Bilko be put on a regimen of light activity, the use of the staff car, card games, selling raffles and running dances.

30. RECRUITING SERGEANT 17/4/56

A wartime buddy, whose life Bilko has saved in battle, calls him with a tip on a 40–1 horse. Colonel Hall is going to Topeka to supervise army enlistment. To leave Bilko alone in camp for two days is courting disaster, so the colonel insists that Bilko accompany him and be in charge of the enlistment booth. Bilko is delighted. He works very hard to keep prospective enlistees from disturbing him while he finds a bookmaker. The colonel checks Bilko's progress and finds – none! Bilko is told he must have five enlistees and goes into scam-mode – in no time he has five recruits. Bilko, followed by his brood,

'The Physical Checkup'

finds the bookmaker. Bilko gets his bet down. The police raid the place. Everyone in the betting rooms, including The Sarge, the enlistees, the bookmaker and his people, is pulled in. The chief of police, dismayed to find his son among the arrested, is worried what the papers will say. Bilko has the solution. Next day Bilko turns over *ten* enlistees – his five, the bookmaker and his cohorts. Bilko's horse, sad to say, did not win.

31. THE BARBER SHOP (a.k.a. HAIR) 24/4/56

Bilko tries to date WAC Master Sergeant Lily Watkins. She turns him down because she has found a handsome corporal with a beautiful head of hair. Bilko looks for solace at the base barber shop where Tony has been trying to cure the trickster's baldness for seven years. Tony is certain that he has finally concocted an elixir that will make the crop grow. Tony massages his treatment into Bilko's head, sets up a heat lamp and leaves for lunch. Bilko falls asleep. Sergeants Sowici and Mullen sneak into the shop and glue a crew-cut hairpiece on Bilko's bare noggin. Bilko awakens and shows Tony the miracle. Tony wants to put his product on the market and orders supplies. Bilko goes back to the barracks and shampoos his new growth. Hot water loosens the hairpiece. Bilko is still bald. Tony has put all his savings – $300 – into supplies. Bilko tells Pendelton and company that the money has come from a widow and a blind man. The contrite three are sucked in by Bilko's fiction and give Tony $350. Tony makes a profit.

32. THE CON MEN 1/5/56

Doberman has received $500 from an insurance company in settlement of an accident claim. Doberman asks Bilko to invest it for him. Bilko is tempted but cannot cheat Doberman with the big, soulful eyes.

Doberman cashes the cheque in town and then goes to meet Bilko in the hotel across the street. Two men and a woman who pretend they are from Doberman's home town immediately spot Doberman's large roll of cash. A game of poker is started. Doberman's money is soon gone. Doberman returns to the barracks and tells his sad story. Bilko goes after the sharpies. Dressed in a creased uniform and a sloppy hat he goes to the same hotel, flashes a roll and, in no time, is involved with the same con people who had fleeced Doberman. Bilko soon has all their money. A gun is pulled, but the door opens and the entire platoon is standing there. The sharpies give up the gun and leave town.

33. WAR GAMES 8/5/56

A group of new recruits is assigned to Bilko for basic training. To Bilko, basic training is learning how to deal from the bottom of the deck. He turns the training over to one of the recruits who has been to military school. The young GI does a great job of instilling military skills in his charges. He also indoctrinates them into believing that the Slippery Sergeant is a great leader and must be followed in every martial situation. Bilko is best man at a wedding on the same night that the annual war games start. The 'enemy' is a National Guard regiment. Bilko, dressed in civilian finery, heads for the wedding followed by the eager-beaver recruits who assume that he is leading them into mock battle. Colonel Hall follows the recruits. They 'invade' the wedding with rifles aimed at the guests. They take the bride's father, who is captain of the National Guard regiment, prisoner, thereby winning the war games.

34. BILKO IN WALL STREET 15/5/56

Bilko is scheduled to go on furlough to New York and he recalls that his wartime buddy, Morgan Twinhazy, works on Wall Street. He writes to him. Twinhazy's reply, on elegant paper with the name Butterworth, Butterworth and Butterworth deeply engraved, prompts Bilko to conclude that Twinhazy is a mover and shaker on Wall Street. Twinhazy invites Bilko to stay with him. He wants his old sarge to see Bermuda. Bilko convinces himself that Morgan has a yacht and is asking him to visit Bermuda. Arrival in New York and disenchantment. Morgan, his wife and baby (whose name is Bermuda) live way below the poverty line. Twinhazy, a head bookkeeper, receives $42 a week. The Butterworths are still living in the nineteenth century. The trickster manipulates the Butterworth firm and a potential client of theirs to believe in Morgan's importance to their operations. Morgan Twinhazy ends up with $250 a week.

Season Two 1956/1957

35. PLATOON IN THE MOVIES 18/9/56

An army film crew arrives at the motor pool at Fort Baxter. They're making a film about keeping sludge out of spark plugs. They need a GI to act the part of Private All-Thumbs. Doberman is chosen. Duane acts like a star, demanding more lines and a stand-in. Every time the camera is pointed at him and the lights are turned on, Doberman reacts like the true professional he is – he faints. Finally the director shuts down the production and leaves the camp. Bilko is left in charge of getting the gear packed and stowed. The cameraman and lighting technician look to him for orders. Bilko turns the training film into a Hollywood spectacle with singing and dancing WACs and skimpy costumes. 'Sludge' is a

'Platoon in the Movies'

sexy dancer and Bilko sings, 'There's a lot of spark left in the old sparkplug tonight.' A general and his wife see the finished film. Mrs General loves the work and the General calls to congratulate Bilko.

36. ITS FOR THE BIRDS 25/9/56

A marine and a sailor have both won the famous quiz programme, *The $64,000 Question*. Only the army has not had a winner. Bilko looks for a suitable contestant . . . someone with encyclopedic knowledge about one subject. A great deal of money is involved but that has nothing to do with Bilko's search. The honour of the army is at stake. Finally, he discovers an expert on birds in his own platoon, Pvt Honnergar: Honnergar is so knowledgeable because he was stationed all alone for eighteen months in an Arctic weather station, where the only reading matter was *Weiscopf's Complete Bird Book*. Honnergar has read the book dozens of times, and even the mention of the book makes him violently ill. It is the final night of the quiz. Honnergar has agreed to go for the $64,000 question. Bilko is in the isolation booth helping Honnergar. The climax is too dramatic to be revealed here.

37. BILKO GOES TO COLLEGE 2/10/56

At Schmill, a 'schmall' University, Bilko is instructing the R.O.T.C.* in the care and feeding of military vehicles. The dean asks the Sarge to use army discipline on a student who has run up a gambling debt with a local bookie. Bilko attempts to make a deal with the bookie; the bookie bad-mouths Bilko and the student. Bilko seeks revenge. Schmill's anorexic football team plays Nôtre Dame every year and always gets beaten by at

* Reserve Officer's Training Corp

least 100–0. Bilko gives the bookie a hundred-dollar bill and places a thousand-to-one bet that Schmill will beat Nôtre Dame. Bilko's public-relations campaign publicises the non-fact that every Schmill player weighs at least 250 pounds. The bookie has second thoughts. If he loses, he will be out by one hundred thousand dollars. He tries to settle his bet with Bilko for a few thousand dollars. Bilko will have none of it. Schmill loses to Nôtre Dame by 99–1. It is considered a great victory for Schmill. For the first time, their arch rival has scored less than a 100 points against them.

38. THE GIRL FROM ITALY 9/10/56

New York. Even though no tickets are available for *My Fair Lady* for months, Bilko, Henshaw and Rocco Barbella scam seats. Rocco calls home and finds out that the girl his brother is supposed to marry has just arrived from Italy. Despite the fact that he has been engaged to Rosa since he was born, Angie refuses to marry her because she looks too old-country. Rocco has to go home. His parents and the girl are distraught. Ernie goes along to help. Taking his cue from the plot of *My Fair Lady*, Bilko decides to pull a Henry Higgins and make the peasant into a beauty. He gets Rosa's hair cut in a stylish do, flimflams a designer out of a gorgeous gown and takes Rosa out. Angie gets reports on what's happening by phone and grows more and more anxious to be with his sudden beloved. When at last he sees her, there is no question that they will be married.

39. THE FACE ON THE RECRUITING POSTER 16/10/56

Mike, a handsome new recruit, is assigned to Bilko's platoon. Bilko takes him to the office to complete his paper work and the WACs fight to get close to him. His charisma is so powerful that Bilko declares himself

Mike's agent. Hollywood will not even look at Mike's photographs. To get publicity, Bilko submits his 'star' for the face on the recruiting poster. Washington instructs Fort Baxter to pick the ten best-looking men in camp and administer a test about military procedure. The soldier with the best test score will be on the poster. Mike is good looking but he's not smart. Doberman is assigned to coach him. The platoon goes to Washington for the test. Bilko and the army brass are dismayed when Doberman wins. No one has the guts to tell Duane that he is too ugly to be on the poster. Bilko has an idea: when five million posters appear, they have Doberman's face on it – but he is wearing a gas mask.

40. BILKO'S WAR AGAINST CULTURE 23/10/56

Bilko and his motor pool are deeply involved – not in army vehicles – but in gambling. The colonel informs Bilko that a special service officer for cultural activities has just arrived. The officer is pretty WAC Lieutenant Roxbury. Signs go up all over the post: 'Art Classes, Music, Poetry' etc. Because of Bilko's admonitions, not one soldier volunteers for any class. Desolated, Lt Roxbury acknowledges defeat and prepares to leave. She has failed her first assignment. Bilko is sorry and insists that she come to the recreation hall because the men want to say goodbye to her. At the hall there is a painting class, with Doberman posing in long underwear with a bow and arrow. There are also poetry and music groups. The lieutenant is pleased. She leaves. Bilko takes a painting off an easel. Underneath is a card with numbered boxes. Doberman shoots an arrow at the card. 'Fifteen' announces the King of Gambling. 'Who has fifteen?'

41. THE SONG OF THE MOTOR POOL 30/10/56

The army starts a new TV show. Bilko has honed the platoon in a medley of Stephen Foster melodies but the scout is not buying the act. The gang is trying to find music that will get them on the show. Paparelli, alone in the shower, sings a lovely tune. This catchy melody could be the basis of 'The Song of the Motor Pool.' Lyrics are easy – music is difficult. Paparelli thinks he wrote the melody. The motor pool can't get another audition. But if the colonel thinks he created the melody, he might use his rank. Elaborate gimmicks. The colonel hears the tune day and night. Convinced that it's his song he calls in some favours. Night of the show. The motor platoon is on directly after the signal corps. They present a new song. After a few seconds, the men of the motor pool realise that the signal corps is singing their melody. The motor pool is forced to do the medley of Stephen Foster songs.

42. BILKO'S ENGAGEMENT 6/11/56

Bilko and the other regulars are involved in their Saturday night poker game. Sgt Fender mentions that his wife objects to his card playing because she never gets to see him. Bilko boasts that he has told Joan, a WAC sergeant whom he has been dating, that he will see her after the game. With much machismo, he assures his colleagues that she will be waiting for him. Sgt Henshaw remarks that Joan was in town with a handsome new Fort Baxter sergeant. Bilko is so jealous that he and Joan quarrel. Bilko tries to placate her with a small gift but Doberman mixes up two packages and leaves an engagement ring on Joan's desk. The word about the 'engagement' quickly spreads. From the colonel down, everyone at Fort Baxter congratulates the couple. Bilko struggles, but he is firmly hooked. Joan turns him loose

'The Song of the Motor Pool'

because she does not want to be engaged because of Doberman's error. She wants a ring that was meant for her. The punchline of the show is typical Bilko.

43. A MESS SERGEANT CAN'T WIN 13/11/56

Mess Sergeant Rupert Ritzik is leaving the army. He and his wife, Emma, are going to open a luncheonette with the measly $400 he has saved. He does not want Bilko at his farewell party; he's afraid of losing his paltry stake. Bilko is hurt by this, and appalled that Ritzik has so little money. He scrapes together another $400 and tries to give it to Ritzik. The mess sergeant and Emma won't touch it – they figure that Bilko is just pulling another con. Ernie figures that the only way Ritzik will take the money is if he wins it betting with Sergeant Shrewd, so Bilko sets up a series of sure-to-lose bets with Rupert. Bad luck, Ritzik manages to screw things up so that *he* always loses. Finally, Bilko bets Ritzik that the mess sergeant's name is *not* Rupert Ritzik. At last Rupert has won. Winning the bet has restored the mess sergeant's confidence. He feels that he can now beat Bilko at his betting game. Ritzik re-enlists for another four years.

44. DOBERMAN'S SISTER 20/11/56

The platoon is cleaning up, literally! Fort Baxter Day is approaching – the annual time for family visiting. Every visiting sister has to have a date for the weekend. Pictures are exchanged, deals are negotiated. But not for Doberman's sister, Diane. No one has ever seen her and there are no photographs. Zimmerman is the only one without a date. In order to persuade Zimmerman to squire Diane, Bilko makes up Musselman's Law: 'The uglier the brother the prettier the sister.' He also asks Zimmerman to take his beautiful girlfriend, Joan, to the dance. Zimmerman figures that if Bilko is willing to give

'Doberman's Sister'

up Joan, Diane must be sensational. Zimmerman insists on dating Duane's sister. Bilko begins to believe his own rhetoric and talks Zimmerman out of dating Diane. Sergeant Con goes to the bus station to meet the 'gorgeous' woman he envisions. She turns out to be Duane's twin.

45. WHERE THERE'S A WILL 27/11/56

Gregory, now living in Detroit, is a former member of the platoon. He has been informed that his Uncle Abner had left a big house, cars etc. to his cousins. Greg, the favorite nephew, has been left only one dollar and an one-eyed parrot. The attorney explains that there is nothing that can be done legally and, half jokingly, suggests that Gregory find a confidence man who could scam the inheritance back from the cousins. Gregory immediately thinks of Bilko, world-class hustler. Bilko and the platoon smell money and go to Detroit. At Uncle Abner's house they enact a complicated fictitious plot that reveals to the cousins that Uncle Abner supposedly owned an island with buried treasure worth thirty million dollars. The only living thing that knows the name of the island is the parrot. The cousins offer Gregory the house and car in exchange for the parrot. But Gregory, having been exposed to Bilko, is too smart for them. He trades the parrot for a share of the hypothetical proceeds from the island's treasure.

46. BILKO'S TAX TROUBLE 4/12/56

By mistake, the IRS sends Bilko a letter requesting him to drop by for a chat. Bilko is furious – his tiny military income is not subject to tax. Henshaw and Rocco point out that all of his dances, raffles, concerts and benefits had admission charges and therefore should have been reported. Bilko prepares a list of all his activities, with 'proof' that he made no money from them. The Great Bluffer storms into the IRS office complaining of how he – a great patriot – is being treated, and throws his papers on the desk. He has implicated himself. Eighty-seven dances etc. in a single year are enough to rouse suspicions. Bilko, using the platoon and Joan Hogan, gathers boxes and boxes of documents of his 'losses' and floods the IRS office with paper. The officials plead with him to stop. The boxes keep coming. The IRS breathes a sigh of relief when the last document of 1953 is examined. The door opens and the platoon enters bringing in boxes of documents for 1954.

47. MINKS INC. 11/12/56

Bilko has dipped into the welfare fund to make a business investment. The horse lost. He bamboozles the platoon into demanding that he order a pair of breeding mink. They envision thousands of mink waiting to be made into coats, as they all become millionaires. The mink arrive. There isn't the slightest sign of passion between them. The brochure indicates that breeding season is in the spring. It's November in Fort Baxter. The platoon brings flowers, whistles bird calls, hangs a sign that says 1 May. The mink are unimpressed. One of the mink becomes ill and makes strange sounds. They can't take the mink to the medical officer, so Doberman pretends to be ill and makes the sounds that the mink does. The doctor says that the only time he had heard such sounds before was when he was doing research on *non*-breeding mink. Bilko calls the woman who sold them. He asks what can be done; she answers: 'Run an ad – the way I did.'

48. SGT BILKO PRESENTS ED SULLIVAN 18/12/56

Auditions are being held for the *Ed Sullivan Variety Show*, an annual tribute to the army. Bilko – who will try anything to get out of Fort Baxter – is an aspiring baritone. He is cut off after one note. At a production meeting, Sullivan goes over the army cast and observes that no GI from the Midwest is represented. A jeep is scheduled to come on stage and it needs a driver. Since Fort Baxter is in the Midwest, a telegram is sent to Bilko, the sergeant of the motor pool. Bilko thinks this is a tribute to his singing. When he arrives at rehearsal, he convinces the orchestra leader, the director, and the arranger that Sullivan takes credit for their work. Sullivan finds his creative staff in revolt. Sullivan opens his show and explains that, because of problems, the army show has been cancelled. In its place is a salute to the navy. A group of singing sailors march on stage. At the end of their line – Bilko in navy uniform.

49. BILKO GETS SOME SLEEP 25/12/56

Fort Baxter is fed up with Bilko: the colonel because his jeep hasn't been fixed and Bilko's reports are never filed; Sgt Joan Hogan because he lies to her; and the platoon because he has milked them dry and no one has any money. The guys won't play poker. Bilko is forced to go to bed at ten o'clock. He dreams that his conscience and his ego are fighting over him. Bilko confides to Captain Adams, the psychiatrist, that he can't sleep. The doctor tells Bilko, that if he straightens up, stops conning people and does the work the army pays him for, he will be able to sleep. Bilko changes. He is sweet, considerate, truthful and does his job. Platoon member after platoon member comes to see the psychiatrist. They are all worried because Bilko has changed so much that no one is sure what new nefarious act he has planned.

'Sgt Bilko Presents Ed Sullivan'

50. THE BLUE BLOOD OF THE BILKOS 8/1/57

The captain of the Princeton football team is about to be married to the heiress to the Wingate fortune. The Wingates are one of the snootiest Philadelphia families. The father of the groom is Sergeant Bensonhurst of Fort Baxter. A sergeant attending their daughter's wedding? Impossible! Bilko is furious at the insult to sergeants and descends on the Wingate mansion. He gives the impression that he is secret service. The Wingates are being checked out because Bensonhurst is so high in the government that his security must be protected. Father Wingate has contacted a general in Washington who exposes Bilko for what he is and, at the same time, chastises the Wingates for their attitude toward Sgt Bensonhurst. Father Wingate may have been a major general in World War Two but he was only a corporal in World War One. And no one knows where Grandpa got the title Commodore. At the wedding, Sgt Bensonhurst, in uniform, walks down the aisle with his son.

51. LOVE THAT GUARDHOUSE 15/1/57

Ritzik is cleaned out again by Bilko. Bilko advises Ritzik to give up gambling because he's so bad at it. Ritzik refuses – he contends that he is a great gambler with a run of bad luck. Bilko suggests that Ritzik go to Las Vegas and bet all his money on the roulette wheel. When he is cleaned out he will be finished gambling for the year. Born-loser Ritzik wants to know what number he should bet. In disgust, Sergeant Hoodwinker suggests 'double zero' At 4 a.m., Emma Ritzik awakens Bilko demanding her husband. Rupert is gone. A little detective work reveals that the mess sergeant has headed for Las Vegas. Rupert returns, jubilant. He has won $1,500 on the first spin. Double zero, of course. Emma begs the colonel to put her husband in the guardhouse because that's the only place Bilko can't get at him. Bilko tries many stratagems to get in the guardhouse. Bilko manages to see Rupert for long enough to win the $1,500 but Bilko's conscience bothers him, and he returns the money to Emma. Emma heads for Las Vegas.

52. SERGEANT BILKO PRESENTS BING CROSBY 22/1/57

Bilko reads that Bing Crosby is crossing the country from Hollywood to New York by car. He figures that 'Der Bingle' must go through Kansas and he feels a super-scam coming on. He calls Everett Crosby, Bing's brother and manager, and cons him into getting Bing to make a stopover at the camp. Sergeant Smooth-Operator sells out the hall. The day of the scheduled appearance he receives a telegram that Crosby won't be coming after all. Desperate, he tries to convert a telegraph messenger, who looks somewhat like Crosby, into an entertainer. The messenger's performing ability is restricted to the poem the 'Wreck of the Hesperus'. On the night of the concert, the pseudo-Crosby has just come on stage and the audience is immediately suspicious. The real Crosby walks in from the back of the hall and the crowd goes wild. When Bilko asks him to sing, Bing recites 'The Wreck of the Hesperus'.

53. BILKO GOES TO MONTE CARLO 29/1/57

Bilko develops a system that beats any roulette wheel. His platoon pushes money at him and urges him to go to Monte Carlo. Bilko's air-force buddies bump generals and run various cons to get him to Europe. Every time he changes a plane, the ground crews push betting money at him. He has a $10,000 bankroll. At the Monte Carlo casino he has second thoughts about risking hard-earned GI money. He goes out on a balcony looking sad. A security guard, thinking he has lost his money and is suicidal, takes him to the manager. The manager does not want an American to kill himself over money. He gives Bilko $10,000 to cover his 'losses'. Playing with the casino's money, Bilko loses it all. Another security guard is on duty and Bilko tries the same routine. Again using the casino's money he loses big. He heads for the balcony again but this time the manager has caught on and throws him out. But Bilko has the original $10,000 to return to the soldiers.

54. BILKO ENTERS POLITICS 5/2/57

Bilko tries to persuade Mayor Burke of Rosedale, Kansas, to build a service centre for the men at Fort Baxter. His Honour refuses to consider it. An election is coming up. Bilko decides to run a reluctant Doberman for mayor. The chairman of Burke's party strikes a deal with Bilko. The men will get their service centre if Doberman is withdrawn. Bilko agrees, but the citizens of Rosedale, seeing a chance to get rid of high-handed Burke, force Bilko and Doberman to continue the campaign. Bilko uses the army's facilities to print leaflets, which are dropped from army planes. He uses tanks and jeeps in political parades. The night before the election, Doberman tells the crowd he cannot run for mayor. The state chairman gloats at Doberman's withdrawal. There is a contest for governor next year and Bilko is considering running one of his men for governor. The men get their service centre even though Doberman has withdrawn.

55. BILKO'S TELEVISION IDEA 12/2/57

The platoon is laughing at the antics of TV comic, Buddy Bickford. His routines involve pie and seltzer. Pvt Whitley is watching in disgust. He has submitted a

'Bilko Enters Politics'

hundred TV ideas that have been turned down. At the advertising agency for the Buddy Bickford Show, executives are seeking a situation comedy for Buddy. Someone suggests Buddy as a soldier. Buddy Bickford and the writers head for Fort Baxter, ostensibly to entertain, but actually to do research. Bilko surmises that Buddy is coming to buy Whitley's script, *Tree Surgeon*. Declaring himself Whitley's agent, Bilko instructs his men that, whatever Bickford says, they are not to laugh. Buddy cannot get a chuckle. Bilko assures the comedian that the problem is his material. This year 'wood' is funny. Bilko visits the dayroom and names trees. The men scream with laughter. Buddy, convinced that he has a hit, sends for the producer to finalise the deal. The producer meets Bilko and understands that he is being conned by a master. He suggests Buddy play a character like Bilko. New York quashes the idea. Too far out.

56. SON OF BILKO 26/2/57

Private Perkins has just been assigned to the platoon: nice-looking kid, polite, well spoken. Rocco and Henshaw want to get rid of him. Six months in the army and he has already been transferred fourteen times. Sergeant Hustler is feeling protective and something about the kid strikes a chord. Perkins is a way-out practical joker. He blows reveille at 1 a.m. Bilko is asleep and Perkins puts a blonde wig and feminine make-up on the old con man. A general comes in and Bilko, in full drag, salutes him. The kid has to go. Bilko prepares a complicated scam in which Doberman appears to be shot by Perkins. To everyone's relief, the kid leaves, then Bilko finds a letter and a package. The letter thanks Bilko for his fatherly treatment of Perkins. The package contains a beautiful music box – Perkins' only memento of his dead father. Bilko plays the music box and, as he listens, the music box explodes.

57. ROCK'N'ROLL ROOKIE 5/3/57

The sensational entertainer Elvin Pelvin has been inducted into the army, and young fans and media people immediately surround him wherever he is stationed. The result is always local chaos. A desperate Pentagon seeks the remotest, least-known army installation so that Elvin can spend his two-year posting in peace and security. Fort Baxter, of course! Since Elvin has mechanical ability, he is assigned to the motor pool under the tender care of Mother Hen Bilko. Bilko immediately senses millions and tries to make money from the young man's fame. An important record executive offers Bilko $10,000 for a recording of Elvin. Wherever Elvin goes he is secretly recorded by Bilko and his cohorts. One day he sings a song about his friends at Fort Baxter. Bilko is so touched by the sentiments expressed in the music that he destroys the recording – and the chance for a $10,000 fee.

58. BILKO'S BLACK MAGIC 19/3/57

Pvt Lester Mendelsohn is assigned to Bilko's tender care. Lester had been stranded on a Pacific Island for many years. He has just collected his back pay, which comes to $7,000 and he loves poker: two virtues that make him a prime target for the Bilker. But Ernie is too late – Lester's excellent qualities have already been discovered by Ritzik and Grover. Bilko is angry at the advantage taken of such a fine young man, to say nothing of beating him to the loot. Ritzik has been fascinated by comic books describing voodoo so Bilko decides to use that as his weapon to punish Grover and Ritzik. When drums are heard during the night the two sergeants panic.

'Rock'n'Roll Rookie'

Bilko advises them that a chicken bone necklace and other sacrifices might propitiate the angry god Gumbo. Ritzik and Grover bring gifts to Gumbo, including a pot containing $7,000. Much to everyone's surprise, including his own, Bilko insists that Mendelsohn invest the $7,000 in government bonds.

59. BILKO GOES SOUTH 26/3/57

Fort Baxter is in the grip of a below-zero winter. Bilko figures the only way to get to the warmth of Miami is for the platoon to enter a singing contest being held there. Bilko orders his group to watch for mail from Washington for application forms. An army laboratory in Miami, where a mosquito-borne deadly disease has been discovered, needs human volunteers to be bitten by the insects. He orders that volunteer forms be sent out to the entire army. Bilko's bunch thinks they are applying for the song contest; they are really volunteering for the experiment. Army brass is so impressed with the bravery of the Bilko gang that they put them up in the best Miami hotel. The troops lounge around the pool, work on their tans, enjoy caviar, turkey and champagne, and delight in the curves and conversation of beautiful young women. The mosquito bites prove harmless but the platoon receives a unit citation for courage, to say nothing about a few days in warm weather.

60. BILKO GOES ROUND THE WORLD 2/4/57

Bilko tells Mike Todd, producer of the movie *Around the World in Eighty Days*, that he can go round the world in *eighty hours*. Todd produces advertising that promises $20,000 to the first person who goes round the world in eighty hours. Using air-force contacts, The Flying Con Man arranges a complicated itinerary. Military planes are not allowed to carry passengers so Bilko will travel as a package. Bilko is at the airport waiting to embark on the first leg of the journey, wearing a tag that says PRIORITY EMERGENCY BAGGAGE. MPs ask for his papers and he hides the tag by placing it on a young boy. Two military pilots come rushing in looking for the 'package', grab the boy and take off. The boy's mother is frantic as army communications follow the 'package' from foreign airport to foreign airport. When the plane lands back in Kansas, Mike Todd is there to hand the youngster a cheque for twenty thousand dollars.

61. THE MESS HALL MESS 9/4/57
A magazine runs a contest for the best original American recipe. The prize is $50,000. Sergeant Ritzik's terrible cooking has gotten worse. He is experimenting on the troops as he seeks a speciality to enter in the competition. The hungry GIs have been eating off base. Bilko, Ritzik and Grover wander into a French restaurant and are served a stew that is wonderful. They try to get the recipe from the chef, but he is willing to die rather than give up his family's secret. So, Bilko brings the entire platoon to the restaurant where they empty their stew dishes into an army pot. Bilko then invites the chef to visit the company kitchen. He tastes what is in the pot. His family has betrayed him. For generations they have protected a secret that is *no secret*. A quick reading of the army cookbook reveals that there is actually a recipe identical to the chef's. Bilko suggests to the chef that he should change the name of his restaurant to The Daniel Boone Room and feature 'Kentucky Hunter's Stew'.

62. THE SECRET LIFE OF SERGEANT BILKO 16/4/57
Sleazy journalist Ray Parker has been writing about the 'leaks' in army security. He has come to Fort Baxter because he thinks that he can wine and dine the yokel

'The Mess Hall Mess'

troops and get proof of his allegations. Bilko (no yokel he) and cohorts spot him from pictures in the papers. Bilko tells the colonel that he has invited Parker to be a guest in the barracks so that he will write positive stories about Fort Baxter. Bilko makes sure that all kinds of ordinary reports and blueprints are seen by Parker. The newspaperman pays heavy dollars for every piece of paper. To further confuse the journalist, Bilko turns the platoon into a secret Nazi-like organisation. Their immediate assignment: blow up the Pentagon. Parker is sure he will be killed if he doesn't cooperate. He calls his editor, who comes in by the next plane. Bilko sees to it that the editor is arrested at the airport. The New York paper prints a laudatory article about the fine facility that is Fort Baxter.

63. RADIO STATION WBBH 23/4/57

The radio station in Rosedale, Kansas, can't make a financial go of it and announces it's going off the air. Sergeant Opportunist figures he can make money out of the situation. He persuades friends in the signal corps to tune a transmitter to the same frequency as the about-to-be-defunct station and 'borrow' all the needed GI equipment to run a broadcast operation. Talent includes Doberman as a newscaster and Grover as an unstopp-able Irish tenor. The mess sergeant does a cooking show using recipes for five hundred portions of each dish. The station has no studio, so talent and technicians run from place to place for the broadcasts. They're broadcasting from the colonel's home when he returns unexpectedly. They run out leaving a microphone turned on. Dialogue between the colonel and his wife is heard all over town and turns out to be the funniest soap opera ever heard. Bilko and gang give up broadcasting because they can't take the physical pace.

64. BILKO, THE MARRIAGE BROKER 30/4/57

Lieutenant Tom Wallace takes over as commander of Company B. He declares the motor pool platoon a disaster, and within minutes he has everyone out of bed doing callisthenics. In short order they're on a twenty-mile hike. Three weeks later the hard-worked platoon is desperate and exhausted. None of Bilko's famous jive has worked with the steely officer. Bilko figures that what the young officer needs is romance – a young woman in his life. So Bilko lines up every available female for miles around but Lt Wallace brushes them off. Lieutenant Rogers, a lovely young woman, arrives. For once, Bilko is out of the loop. He does not know that the Lieutenants are secretly engaged but have put off marriage because of family objections. They pretend to be very cold to each other but find they can't wait any longer and order Bilko to get them a jeep so that can go get married.

65. BILKO ACRES 7/5/57

Troops at Fort Baxter are being shipped out to Malaysia or Hawaii or maybe Singapore. Bilko's take on the gossip: just the army's way to confuse. He is certain that the plan is to expand the base. The platoon buys 25 acres of swampland abutting the camp from a local real-estate agent. Bilko is sure the army will buy it from them. Washington orders the camp size to be reduced. Bilko renames the swamp Paradise Acres and offers it to civilians. Sergeant Land-Developer discovers that the mosquitoes are very bad in the area. Bilko tells Doberman to find out what to do – and do it. The real-estate agent has visited Paradise Acres and found oil on his shoes. He tries to buy back the land. Bilko has also discovered oil on *his* shoes. A contract between the agent and the platoon is about to be signed when Doberman blurts out that he has sprayed the swamp with oil to get rid of the mosquitoes.

66. THE BIG SCANDAL 14/5/57

Bilko learns hypnotism from a book. He bets Ritzik that he can hypnotise him. Bilko suggests that Ritzik is madly in love with Nell Hall, the colonel's wife. Ritzik laughs and walks away with the bet. Bilko does not realise that, in the back of the room, Doberman has been hypnotised. Nell is at home packing. She is leaving in a little while to spend time with her family. Bilko comes by to help with the luggage. He picks up the phone and a voice declares its love for Nell. Bilko does not realise that it is Doberman on the phone. He is sure that Nell is leaving the colonel for a phantom lover. Wanting to show Nell that the colonel is still a charmer, Bilko brings in a maid to take care of the house while Mrs Hall is gone. Mrs Hall gets one look at the attractive 'maid' and refuses to leave.

67. BILKO'S PERFECT DAY 21/5/57

Bilko wakes unhappy: the day before he lost bets on 26 races, he was in an accident with the colonel's car, etc. His theory is that the smarter you are, the unluckier you are; that law of nature was promulgated to keep the intelligent from ruling the world. Suddenly he realises that today is perfect: he gets the only hot shower in the platoon; he predicts the number of jelly beans in a jar; when the man whose car he had damaged complains, a lieutenant testifies that he had been with Bilko until after midnight; the bookmaker who was dunning Bilko is hit by a truck. Bilko calculates that his luck will last until midnight so he wants to take advantage of the remaining few minutes of his perfect day. He puts all his money on a horse in Australia. His horse leads by 40 lengths.

Midnight arrives and the horse stumbles. Bilko looks heavenward as he concedes his perfect day is over.

68. THE COLONEL BREAKS PAR 28/5/57

The colonel has changed his vacation plans. Bilko is stuck with gambling arrangements, food concessions and shoddy souvenirs that he was going to peddle during the colonel's absence. He tries to persuade the colonel to enter the army golf tournament in Palm Springs. The colonel is a terminal duffer and refuses to go. Bilko gets his buddy, champion golfer Sam Snead, to work a scam. Bilko is 'coaching' the colonel on the golf course. He instructs the colonel to close his eyes and, as he starts his swing, Snead steps out of hiding, hits the ball and hides again. The colonel ends up eleven under par. He registers in the tournament. Bilko won't let his boss be embarrassed. He takes him on a final practice round, confident that the colonel will reachieve his dufferdom. The colonel plays a great game – with his eyes closed and without Sam Snead.

69. SHOW SEGMENTS 4/6/57

On a rehearsal break, Phil Silvers and some of the actors in the show are having lunch at Lindy's restaurant. Ed Sullivan joins them. They talk about great scenes in previous shows that have been cut because of time constraints. Some funny but deleted moments are shown. One is the famous scene of the baritone Bilko auditioning for the Ed Sullivan show and then being brushed off. Bilko, when he realises he has not made it as a singer, tries to impress the audition officer by telling him that Jan Peerce [a very famous opera singer] and Elvis Presley have begged him to appear. When that doesn't work, Sergeant Stage-Struck tries card tricks, impressions and dancing. In another segment, using

'The Colonel Breaks Par'

fake headlines and phoney radio broadcasts, Bilko and Ritzik try to out-scam each other when betting on an important football game. Another deletion involves Bilko auctioning off souvenirs, including photographs of the Eiffel Tower, which he hints are pornographic, and Hitler's helmet.

70. HIS HIGHNESS DOBERMAN 11/6/57

Dirty Duane is taking a shower – of his own volition. The astounded platoon follows him and discovers that he is dating Lillian, the daughter of a wealthy factory owner. When Lillian introduces her beau to her parents, her mother throws Duane out of the house because he's just a 'common soldier'. Bilko, dressed as a diplomat and wearing a monocle, convinces Lillian's parents that Doberman is a crown prince. He permits her parents to make a small reception for His Highness. Bilko instructs the enthusiastic parents and guests on how to sing the national anthem: *Hail to Crown Prince Doberman*. The reception is in full swing. Captain Barker enters. He has discovered the con and wants to expose Doberman. Lillian tells the captain that Duane has told her that he was born in Allentown, Pennsylvania, and has never been out of the US. Bilko also does his persuasive best and the captain allows the party to go on.

Season Three 1957/1958

71. BILKO'S MERRY WIDOW 17/9/57

The snooty ladies of Rosedale offer a $500 bonus to any producer who will bring a professional theatrical production to their town. Bilko reads about the offer and tries to get rights for a Broadway hit. He is turned down by *My Fair Lady*, *South Pacific* and *Damn Yankees*. Bilko decides on Lehar's *Merry Widow*. Its great virtue is that it's out of copyright. Posing as Max Steinhart, a Broadway impresario, Bilko convinces the ladies that he can produce a professional *Merry Widow*. Bilko's definition of professional is using the platoon and the WACs on the post as talent. The WACs put themselves on sick call in order to rehearse. The colonel finds out. The female soldiers are sent back to their duties. Bilko infiltrates a local finishing school and cons the headmistress into permitting her genteel students to participate instead. The father of one of the girls visits a rehearsal and sees the young ladies in cancan costumes. Back to school, girls! In desperation, Bilko enlists the women performers of a local burlesque house to grace his *Merry Widow*.

72. BILKO'S BOY TOWN 24/9/57

Bilko and his platoon are anxious to go on desert manoeuvres for two weeks. The desert is not just a sandy place – it's on the way to Las Vegas. Colonel Hall catches on and orders the motor pool to guard Fort Baxter while the rest of the troops are away. Bilko persuades some local parents to send their boys to camp: $125 for two weeks. The hustle is working well and the kids are having a good time. Bilko is informed that the colonel and troops are returning to Baxter because of a sandstorm. Sergeant Head Counsellor returns the boys to their parents and refunds part of the tuition. The kids have sworn a mighty Indian Brave oath that they will never reveal what happened at summer camp. One smart youngster can't be returned home because his parents have gone away for a week. The parents finally arrive and the young man tells his story. He lies like Bilko, only better. Each lie costs Bilko serious money.

73. HILLBILLY WHIZ 1/10/57

The motor pool baseball team takes a 24–0 beating from Platoon A. Bilko is furious. The team needs a pitcher. A new man is assigned to them: a hillbilly [played by Dick Van Dyke] who can pitch with either arm, with stunning accuracy. His name is Harry Lumpkin. Bilko gets the New York Yankees interested and takes the platoon to Yankee Stadium for a tryout. The Yankees offer Lumpkin $125,000. He is reluctant to sign because of the team's name. How can a good ol' southern boy pitch for the Yankees? Some of the actual players pretend to be southerners and he signs. His girlfriend Emily, a beautiful hillbilly, pressures him to return home and marry her. At the age of 16 she's afraid of being an old maid. Bilko tears up the contract. A little while later the platoon is watching the Yankees on TV. Lumpkin is pitching flawless ball and Emily is broadcasting the play-by-play.

74. BILKO'S VALENTINE 8/10/57

Sergeant Joan Hogan is furious that Bilko has forgotten to send her a Valentine's Day card. She does not want to see Bilko again. Her hitch in the army is up. She doesn't re-enlist; she returns home. Bilko is broken hearted and tries to phone Joan. She refuses to talk to him. Bilko gets himself a temporary transfer to the WAC enlistment unit. He arranges to be stationed in Joan's home town and has parades pass her house. He makes a speech, ostensibly to a crowd of young women, but he is actually pleading with Joan. She pays no attention. He rings the doorbell and gets the door slammed in his face. Joan dreams she has re-enlisted to serve in Europe. She dreams of meeting a man in Paris – he is Bilko; a handsome Italian – he is Bilko; a suave gentlemen in London – he is Bilko. She gives up and re-enlists. On her first

'Hillbilly Whiz'

day back, Ernie brings her flowers, candy, perfume and sweetly calls her . . . Helen!

75. THE BIG MANHUNT 15/10/57

In South Africa, Red Thompson has just discovered a huge diamond mine. During a battle fifteen years ago, Bilko had saved Red's life. Thompson had sworn to share any good fortune that came his way with Bilko. He sets investigators to search for Bilko but doesn't release Bilko's name to the press for fear of being inundated with impostors. Back at Fort Baxter, Kansas, Bilko is having big problems raising the bus fare to Topeka where the Poker Olympics are being held. When he reads about the diamond mogul seeking to find him he heads for New York City. At Red's hotel a long line of would-be-heroes is filling Thompson's suite. When Bilko and Red finally meet there is great rejoicing. The generous Mr T hands Bilko a signed cheque and tells Bilko to fill in any amount he wishes. Bilko writes a seven-figure number. One of Thompson's partners rushes in. Their diamond mine is on someone else's property. Bilko gives Red a hundred dollars to help tide him over.

76. BILKO'S DOUBLE LIFE 22/10/57

Everyone in Rosedale, Kansas, is after Bilko. He owes money to his bookie, all the restaurants, the jeweller for a bracelet he bought for Joan – the list of Bilko pursuers is long. He escapes Fort Baxter and heads for New York. In the big city, Herbert Penfield III, Bilko's exact double [no wonder, he is played by Phil Silvers] seeks a small town where he hopes to be appreciated for himself, not his money. Bilko goes to a swank hotel in New York where he is taken for Penfield and his every whim is catered for. Penfield comes to Rosedale, is called Bilko and dunned by everyone. He keeps paying off Bilko's creditors. In New York Bilko goes to a Penfield family meeting being run by a rapacious uncle. He gets his double, the real Penfield, elected president of the family trust and saves their fortune. Bilko returns to Rosedale just as Penfield is heading back for New York. They recoil as they recognise each other.

77. SERGEANT BILKO PRESENTS 29/10/57
Pvt Hugo Lockman has written a play that is being produced by the local junior high school. An assistant principal remarks that Lockman's work is as good as that of Tennessee Williams [the famous American playwright]. Bilko appoints himself Lockman's agent. He looks for funding to stage the play properly. When he can't find backers he decides the army should come up with production money. Bilko shows the special services major every member of his platoon busy at typewriters. They're all writing plays. The major is conned into initiating an army contest for aspiring playwrights. Bilko expects Lockman to be the only entrant. Bilko hands Lockman's finished play to Doberman. Duane is instructed to address the envelope and put it in a mailbox. The special services officer announces that there were 750 GIs who entered the contest. The winner is a corporal in Oklahoma. The officer wonders why no one from Bilko's platoon entered the contest since they were all writing plays. No one had told Doberman to put stamps on the envelope.

78. PAPA BILKO 5/11/57
France 1944. Bilko brings food to a French family whom he has befriended. His favourite is a seven-year-old girl, Mignon. She calls Ernie 'Papa Bilko'. Fast forward to 1957, camp Baxter. Everybody in camp pays homage to Pearly Johnson, a man who makes girls' hearts throb.

Pearly has an address book with hundreds of names in it – organised by hair colour, height, complexion and looks. Mignon, now beautifully grown up, comes to base headquarters looking for Papa Bilko. It is explained that 'Papa' is a term of endearment – not a description of a relationship. Mignon stays at the Ritzik house. Pearly Johnson gets one look at Mignon and begins courting her. Bilko is upset because he still thinks of her as a little girl and of Pearly as a womaniser. He wants to scare Pearly off. Carrying a rifle, Bilko informs Pearly that he has to marry Mignon. Pearly and Mignon couldn't be happier. Bilko gives his blessing. As the ceremony is about to start Pearly hands Bilko his address book. Joan immediately appropriates it.

79. BILKO TALKS IN HIS SLEEP 19/11/57

Bilko has a date with a gorgeous girl. He has promised her dinner at the most expensive restaurant in the Fort Baxter area. Slight problem. His assets are zero and those of the platoon are ditto. He sets up all sorts of gambling gimmicks to gather in what he can. The old 'count the beans in the jar' and the equally ancient 'on whom will the fly land?' scams. Grover and Ritzik come to Bilko's room. He is talking in his sleep and reveals the secrets of the gimmicks. They win the money. When Sergeant Sleeping-Loud-Mouth realises what has happened he feigns sleep and Grover and Ritzik hear that he has but three months to live. He reckons they will pity him and return the money. Grover and Ritzik send for one of the best doctors in the country. They have spent the $300 they won to bring the doctor to save Bilko's life.

80. CHEROKEE ERNIE 26/11/57

The platoon is going on furlough. Money that Bilko had been holding for them was eaten by a racehorse. White

Eagle, a new recruit, suggests that Bilko can make back the money in Tulsa. Oil workers are always looking for a game. White Eagle invites Ernie to stay at his house. White Eagle's father is a successful rancher with a home to match. The Bureau of Indian Affairs has redirected the water supply so that the ranch is cut off. In order to plead the Eagle's case, Bilko is inducted into the Cherokees and named Bald Eagle. He discovers a document that indicates that all of Oklahoma belongs to the Cherokees. Negotiations. The Scheming Sergeant wants $50 million. A local professor declares the treaty valid. The historical museum buys the treaty document and the Cherokees use that money to buy adjacent land that has water. The platoon is invited to take its furlough at the ranch.

81. BILKO BUYS A CLUB 3/12/57
Bilko tries to buy a small piece of land with a decrepit building just outside Fort Baxter. He plans to build a club with gaming rooms in the back. He needs $750 for the down payment. As usual, everyone around Bilko is tapped out. A national guard contingent is in for two weeks of training. Bilko is told that one of the national guardsmen is involved in a five-million dollar deal. But which one? Bilko's intuition picks a butcher whom he treats royally. The real millionaire is put on kitchen and latrine duty. Bilko takes the national guard members out to view the land, explaining that he wants the tract for an old soldiers' home. Later, at the barracks, the chaplain shows Bilko a cheque from the real millionaire who was so impressed with Bilko's pitch that he donated $20,000. Bilko gets credit for the idea; the chaplain keeps the cheque for the soldier's home.

'Cherokee Ernie'

82. LIEUTENANT BILKO 10/12/57

Bilko's hitch is up and he won't re-enlist. Colonel Hall is very happy; the platoon is sad. When he is being processed out, it is discovered that, during battle, Bilko was promoted to lieutenant. The order was never rescinded. The honour does not mean much to Bilko, but the $20,000 back pay means a great deal. He is now an officer. A general suggests that Bilko make the first manned balloon flight 30 miles into the stratosphere. If a general *suggests*, one obeys. Bilko is a reluctant flyer and is delighted when the project goes back to the drawing board. Because officers have to pay for rent, food and uniform, master sergeants are much better off financially than lieutenants are. Captain Barker calculates Bilko's back pay which means Bilko still owes the army $6,000. When Bilko hears this, he releases his commission. The colonel, believing that Bilko is leaving the army, is upset when he discovers that Sergeant Sharpie has re-enlisted.

83. BILKO AT BAY 17/12/57

Bilko, Rocco and Henshaw are headed for New York in Bilko's car. They're short of money. They route themselves to the homes of members of the platoon. They bring news of the GI and cadge a meal. The hungry trio arrives at Mrs Doberman's tourist house in Altoona, Pennsylvania. Staying at the house are two 'fisherman' who are waiting for their friend Louie. The car breaks down and Bilko and cohorts stay overnight. Bilko reads in the paper that bank robbers are being sought. Mrs Doberman goes out to a garden club meeting. Bilko senses that the two boarders are the bank robbers. His suspicions are confirmed when the robbers pull guns. Louie arrives. The outlaws are heading out when cops arrest them. Mrs Doberman has called them – she knew all along that the fishermen were criminals. Bilko asks her why she waited so long to call the police. She answers that she was waiting for Louie.

84. BILKO F.O.B. DETROIT 24/12/57

Colonel Hall has sent the motor pool to Detroit to pick up new trucks at the factory. He has ordered Bilko to return in two days. In the past, Bilko has managed to take a week to get back to base. Bilko inspects the vehicles and finds the wheelbase is out a $\frac{1}{16}$ of an inch (the truck specs allow $\frac{1}{8}$ of an inch tolerance), and other minor discrepancies. His aim, of course, is to delay his return while the factory makes adjustments. The scamster sells the president of the company on his Basic Training Kit. With this kit new recruits can do their basic training in their own backyards and report for service fully trained, saving the government millions of dollars. A general visits the factory and reveals that Bilko's Basic Training Kit has been turned down six times. Bilko faces Colonel Hall's wrath – which is increased when Bilko admits that he has returned without the new trucks.

85. BILKO AND THE FLYING SAUCERS 31/12/57

Bonnie Morgan calls Bilko from Washington where she is performing at a club. It's been fourteen years since they have seen each other on New Guinea where he was stationed and she was a singer with the USO (United Service Organisation). Bilko is eager to get to DC to see her. He reads a bulletin which instructs all personnel to report sightings of flying saucers to the Pentagon. Bilko realises that, if *he* makes such a report, it will be viewed with suspicion – especially by the nervous major who is temporary commanding officer. Using balloons and a tape recorder he fools some of his men into believing that they have seen saucers. They report this. That

'Bilko and the Flying Saucers'

night, the major, inspired by balloons, tape recordings and Doberman dressed as a spaceman, also sees saucers. Instead of sending Bilko to the Pentagon, an investigator is sent to Fort Baxter. Bilko, Doberman and friends end up in the locked ward of the base hospital for 'observation'.

86. BILKO AND THE COLONEL'S SECRETARY 7/1/58

The colonel's secretary has been reassigned. She had been good to Bilko and his boys: no tough jobs for the motor platoon. After checking the records of every available candidate from all over the country, Bilko feels that Cpl Blanche Ripley is just the kind of secretary the colonel needs. The day before, Blanche had found her true love and the next morning she is transferred hundreds of miles away to Fort Baxter. Bilko boasts that he arranged the transfer. She is furious. She sees to it that Bilko and his group are assigned to garbage detail, painting assignments, furnace room cleanups. Bilko can't get rid of her. He persuades the colonel that Blanche is in love with him, despite the difference in their ages. The colonel panics and has her transferred back to her original assignment. He wants a new secretary: a man. The colonel gets his male secretary. He is Blanche's boyfriend. The lovers are once again separated by many miles because of Bilko's machinations. There is no doubt that the new secretary will seek vengeance.

87. DOBERMAN, THE CROONER 14/1/58

Bilko hears a home-made recording that sends the feel of big money coursing through his veins. A mellow baritone sings 'Annie Laurie' with beauty and emotion. Bilko will make the soldier/singer a big star – if he can find out who he is. The sarge scours the post for the mystery man. The singer turns out to be Doberman. Bilko sets an audition with a record company. Duane admits that he only makes those glorious sounds when he has a cold; when he is healthy, his voice sounds like he looks. The schemer tries many ways to give Duane a cold. Duane can't even work up a sneeze. At the base hospital the doctor is inoculating volunteers with a cold virus so he can test the efficacy of a cold vaccine. Bilko volunteers Doberman. The doctor announces that Duane responded very well to the vaccine – now he is the only man in the country immune to colds.

88. BILKO PRESENTS KAY KENDALL 21/1/58
Kay Kendall was a prominent and very beautiful English actress who made it big in Hollywood playing serious parts.

Kay Kendall is in Rosedale, Kansas, promoting a film. Bilko is promoting *'An Album of American Folk Music'* at Rosedale's Fort Baxter. Sergeant Sleaze has added a creative touch to the old time music – undulating WACs in skimpy costumes. The colonel sees a rehearsal and closes the show down. Bilko is stuck with two hundred dollars' worth of costumes and is desperate to find a place to put on his opus. Bilko sees Kay Kendall at her hotel and pretends to be British army. Kay catches on immediately but she is amused by him and plays along. Ernie invites her to come to a small gathering of Brits that evening and she agrees to put in an appearance. When the theatre owner in town hears the name Kay Kendall, his space is immediately available. That evening, fifteen hundred people are in the audience. Colonel Hall greets the Hollywood star and lets slip that Bilko has been selling tickets to the event. Miss Kendall wants to make sure that the audience gets its money back. When she is introduced, she pretends to be drunk, and Bilko is forced to refund the ticket money. Kendall,

'Doberman the Crooner'

perfectly sober, announces that she will do a scene from *Romeo and Juliet* – with Bilko playing Romeo.

89. BILKO'S COUSIN 28/1/58

Bilko's uncle wires Bilko that his cousin Swifty is on his way to the sergeant's platoon as a new recruit. Bilko is happy to have another Bilko's crafty mind and card-playing hands. Swifty [played by Dick Van Dyke] is not very *swift*. He's sweet, polite and completely innocent of the way the world works. He's the perfect fall guy. Bilko (the con man) realises that Bilko (the yokel) will not make it in the army. He thinks that Swifty might survive as an officer but, despite the sting-master's machinations, Swifty doesn't make officer's training school. Swifty is sent to Mount Wilson, a lonely place with an observatory on top. Swifty is very happy. Goats and sheep are his best friends. Clem Bilko turns up – he is Swifty's brother and everything one could expect from a man named Bilko. He wears a gambler's eyeshade under his cap and shuffles a deck of cards with the skill that has made Bilko a legend.

90. BILKO'S PIGEONS 4/2/58

Bilko has been using the fort's messenger pigeons as a gambling device. The birds are released. Bilko takes bets on which one will be the first to return home. The profits are small but steady. The Pentagon orders that messages are no longer to be sent by pigeon and that all facilities must be disbanded. The colonel warns Bilko that, if he doesn't get rid of the pigeons, he will be broken down to private and sent to Alaska. Bilko discovers that the pigeons are worth real money. He sells the four pigeons he has to George, a rich boy whose hobby is raising pigeons. The pigeons return to Bilko's roost. He sells them again to Ritzik. The pigeons return home. He sells them once more to Grover. The colonel has been receiving calls from George that his pigeons have again disappeared. He comes to Bilko's quarters to check on things himself. As he watches the pigeons return to their roost, Bilko opens his locker and starts putting on Arctic clothing.

91. CYRANO DE BILKO 11/2/58

On behalf of Harold, a shy private, Bilko writes a letter to Natalie Rumpelmeyer of Rosedale. The girl is touched by 'Harold's' flattering prose. Bilko is not aware that there is a second Natalie Rumpelmeyer living in the house: a good-looking but middle-aged aunt. Bilko is sure that this is a case of an older woman trying to entrap a younger man. Harold plans to buy an engagement ring. Bilko is suspicious – things are progressing too fast. Bilko gets involved with the older Natalie. When Harold arrives, Bilko finds out that there is another Natalie. At a surprise party, Bilko and Natalie Sr's engagement is announced. A guest – the local police chief – warns Bilko that, if he doesn't treat Natalie right, Ernie will have to answer to him. Bilko realises that the police chief is in love with Natalie. He prepares a phoney diary showing that Natalie is in love with the police chief. There is a double wedding – the two Natalies marry the men of their choice and Bilko is home free.

92. THE COLONEL'S REUNION 21/2/58

Colonel Hall initiates 'Operation Moonbeam': all-out warfare against gambling. Wherever the card players gather, MPs are there to bust up the games. Bilko is frantic – never before has he been *unable* to outwit the colonel. He needs Hall off the base for a few days. He reads about industrialist and ex-general Whitney having a reunion with old comrades. John Hall has been left off the guest list. Bilko gets Colonel and Mrs Hall invited. He drives them to the reunion and overhears the low regard in which his colonel is held. He may be at war with the colonel, but he's still his colonel. Wearing a trench coat and a black eye patch under his glasses, he convinces Whitney that Colonel Hall is the mastermind and director of super-secret 'Operation Moonbeam', aimed at the enemies of the United States. Whitney, impressed, offers the colonel a job in his firm.

93. BILKO SAVES RITZIK'S MARRIAGE 28/2/58

Ritzik stops by the poker game to announce that he is not playing. It's his fifteenth wedding anniversary and he has to be home. Bilko inveigles him into a hand or two. Ritzik realizes that he is nine hours late for his anniversary dinner. Ritzik and Emma have a flaming row and she leaves home. Ritzik is not unhappy, but Bilko feels guilty that he has broken up a marriage. Emma arrives and hands Rupert a subpoena. She is divorcing him. Pretending to be Ritzik, Bilko goes to the judge's chambers and convinces him not to grant the divorce. His Honour persuades Emma to return home. Rupert and Emma are polite to each other and bored with each other. Ritzik invites Bilko for poker. Emma flares up and they have a big fight. They embrace. Their contentious marriage is back.

94. BILKO, THE ART LOVER 7/3/58

Sergeant Bilko has not been himself. He snaps at the platoon, demands work, and clean barracks. He acts like a sergeant. The troops think Bilko is sick. The doctor diagnoses it as nerves. Bilko gets a two-week furlough. The wangler gets himself invited to Carlisle Thompson's [played by Alan Alda] mansion in New York. Thompson was in the motor pool. He arrives as Carlisle is storming out clutching a statue *Woman and Grapes*. The young man has had a fight with his father. He wants to be a sculptor. The rich kid has no money and takes Bilko along to find a terrible apartment on the Lower East Side. Bilko has come to town for pampering and he is offered poverty. Not Bilko's style. He tries to peddle Carlisle's art and has no takers. The older Mr Thompson buys a new building; Sergeant Slicker persuades him that the lobby needs a statue. Bilko has just the thing. *The Spirit of Transportation*, a.k.a. *Woman and Grapes*. Bilko is given the run of the house. He does not trust himself to be alone with the pretty maid and leaves.

95. BILKO, THE GENIUS 14/3/58

The Pentagon has entered the test scores of all army personnel on punch cards*. Someone wearing spiked golf shoes has stepped on Bilko's card. Bilko is declared a genius and sent to a special camp where high IQ men work on secret projects. Bilko overhears that the brass has discovered the card punched by golf shoes. He will be out of the camp in two days. Determined to profit from the situation, he asks the smart residents if they can predict the winners of horse races. They come up with a formula that forecasts the winners of eight races at Santa Anita. Bilko contacts his bookmaker just a few hours before the first race. The bookmaker insists on cash for the bet. No one leaves 'Camp Genius' without permission so Bilko gets the scientists to dispatch a rocket containing $100 to Fort Baxter. The scientific race card wins. But Bilko's bet was never put down. The money-carrying rocket has been intercepted by Army intelligence.

* Punch cards were used to enter data in early computers.

'Bilko, the Genius'

96. BILKO, THE MALE MODEL 28/3/58

Bilko goes to the Chicago area on military business. Being Bilko, he manages to go out on the town with the leading lady of a Windy City's burlesque house. A picture of him with the lady appears in a national magazine. A New York advertising agency believes that they can sell their client's smoking jacket by using a male model with an average face . . . a Mr Common Man. Bilko's face in the magazine fits their concept and he is tracked down and brought to New York. The ad is prepared and tested – at Bilko's suggestion – in Rosedale, home of Fort Baxter. Bilko sends the platoon, dressed variously as farmer, woodsman and Indian Chief, to buy smoking jackets. The agency is impressed with the reaction and schedules the ad. Zero jackets are sold. The agency investigates why their research was so wrong in Rosedale. They discover they have been scammed. The agency threatens to call the district attorney. End of another promising Bilko career!

97. THE COLONEL'S INHERITANCE 4/4/58

The colonel receives $5,000 in cash, an inheritance. He orders his secretary to get two MPs to escort the money to the bank. Bilko overhears. He gets Rocco and Henshaw to dress as MPs and escort the money to – Bilko. Ernie wants to flash the cash around. His creditors will be impressed with the cash and extend him even more credit. The soldiers go to make the deposit. Bilko overhears a stock tip in the bank. Over the objections of Henshaw and Rocco – and his own conscience – he invests the colonel's money in the stock. In an hour, the bottom falls out of the stock. Bilko has shown his cash to his bookmaker who sets a cardsharp on Sergeant Desperate. Bilko makes back the five thousand. The colonel has heard that a soldier with glasses had been upset about the crash of the stock. He immediately thinks of Bilko. Bilko gives the colonel the deposit slip made out to him. The commanding officer is ashamed of having doubted Bilko.

98.BILKO'S HONEYMOON 11/4/58

The colonel and his wife are going to South Dakota to see her parents. Private Dino Paparelli is an inveterate contestant. He has written the winning slogan for a contest for newly weds run by a Miami Hotel. The prize: a two-week honeymoon for the happy couple. Bilko dresses Paparelli in a WAC uniform, provides him with a blonde wig, and they head for Florida. Colonel and Mrs Hall show up at the hotel – her parents were away from home. They decided to take in some warm weather. Mrs Hall spots Bilko and his 'wife'. Bilko promises that he and his 'wife' will have dinner with them. Paparelli obviously can't go. Bilko shows up with a beautiful, hard-drinking, rough-talking blonde. She turns on Bilko and gives him back his wedding ring. The colonel tells Bilko that his supposed wife is a floozy and, to protect him, he is cancelling the sergeant's leave. He orders him back to Fort Baxter.

99. BILKO'S CHINESE RESTAURANT 25/4/58

When he learns that Wong Lee's father owns ten Chinese restaurants, Bilko takes the new recruit under his tender care. The young man becomes technical adviser to the Scheming Sergeant's venture – a Chinese restaurant. Ritzik, the mess sergeant who can't cook in any language, is put through a crash course in Chinese cuisine. He surprises even himself by mastering Oriental edibles. The Pentagon notices that Ritzik orders large quantities of bamboo shoots, water chestnuts, and rice. They have been looking for new units to send to

Macoochi Atoll. Troops that enjoy such large quantities of Chinese foods should adapt quickly to the prudish culture of Macoochi. An officer arrives to brief them about their new post. Bilko demonstrates the concepts he has for Macoochi: a large electric sign proclaiming CHEZ MACOOCHI, cha-cha dancers, with women well underdressed. The officer arranges not to disturb the serenity of Fort Baxter by moving any of its personnel out.

100. OPERATION LOVE 2/5/58
Because of Bilko's persuasive ways with cards and roulette wheels, the men of Fort Baxter are gambling more and paying less attention to their dates and steady girlfriends. The WACs are fed up and start transferring to other camps. In a matter of six weeks there isn't a WAC left at Fort Baxter. And the men, rightly, blame their lack of female companionship on Bilko. Without women, they're too unhappy to gamble with Ernie. Bilko-the-Shrewd goes to Camp Madison, the central training camp for WACs. In the presence of the women, he receives telephone calls from 'Clark Gable', 'Jimmy Stewart' and others. These luminaries are supposed to be talking from Hollywood – actually they're all the product of Henshaw's mimicry. Bilko and the platoon also record a romantic song about life in Fort Baxter. Word gets around. And soon many WACs have transferred to Fort Baxter. Every GI has an attractive WAC on his arm. Doberman – that charmer – has a WAC on *each* arm. Gambling will start again.

101. BILKO'S TV PILOT 9/5/58
Morgan Montana is an authentic cowboy. He joins the motor pool and annoys everyone with his loud voice and exuberant good cheer. Doberman is the only platoon

'Bilko's TV Pilot'

member who likes him. They become buddies and Doberman has a photograph taken of the two of them in cowboy outfits. Doberman sends the photo to CBS TV. They are willing to talk. Bilko comes to New York to meet with the brass. They are not interested in Morgan but in Doberman. Bilko decides to make his own pilot with Doberman. There is professional film equipment stored with Sergeant J. J. Coogan, who won't release the camera and lights for Bilko's use. Bilko promises Hilda, a chubby, plain waitress, a part in the pilot if she persuades her boyfriend J. J. to let them use the film gear. The Bilko gang makes a pilot, which they show in all its awfulness to the CBS brass. Bilko is disgraced; Hilda is hired to star in the new Western epic being filmed for next season.

102. BILKO RETIRES FROM GAMBLING 16/5/58

If anything, gambling at Fort Baxter has got worse. The colonel calls in a professional cardsharp – a stage performer – who can make cards do anything. He joins a regular platoon game. Bilko loses to Ritzik to the tune of $500. Bilko goes into a complete decline. Overnight he turns into an old man, frightened, fragile. The morale of the platoon, in fact all of Fort Baxter, is undermined. Bilko's attention is called to a newspaper story about the cardsharp, whom he recognises as one of the 'GIs' who sat in on the disastrous game. He wants revenge. He continues to act the depressed soldier. The colonel takes Bilko into his own home and calls in the poker regulars. In minutes, the old Bilko is back winning all the money he has lost, and more. The next morning he escorts a beaten Ritzik into the colonel's office. Ritzik is suffering the same kind of breakdown that had laid Bilko low.

103. BILKO'S VACATION 23/5/58

Bilko has managed to frazzle the colonel's nerves with his antics. The medical officer recommends that the colonel go on vacation and that he should give Bilko and the entire platoon leave at the same time. Bilko makes a deal with Dimmeldorf Lodge. If he gets twenty guests to go to the the Lodge, he will be given a free room. He tells the platoon that there are lots of gorgeous girls at the lodge. He tells Fender, father of six, about a most-beautiful child contest. The colonel finds an ad for Dimmeldorf on his desk – the guests are preparing to leave when they find out they have been tricked. Colonel Hall sends himself a telegram stating that a movie studio would like to start filming at Fort Baxter the next day. Bilko intercepts the telegram (the colonel says that Bilko *always* reads his telegrams first) and heads back to Fort Baxter to make sure that he won't miss making contact with Hollywood big shots. The colonel has shot down the con artist with his own weapons.

104. BILKO'S INSURANCE COMPANY 30/5/58

Realising that there are ten thousand GIs at Fort Baxter, Bilko forms his own insurance company. Total capital: Bilko's shifty brain. He sells every kind of insurance, including a policy with generous benefits for multiple births. He peddles insurance to new recruit Gunther and to WAC Sally. Sally is a triplet, her mother was a triplet; Gunther has a twin. With that kind of heredity their first *child* could be many *children* – enough to wipe out the under-funded insurance company. When Bilko finds out that Gunther and Sally are courting, he is frantic. He tries every ruse that he can think of to keep the two apart, but love outwits Sergeant Schemer and they marry. And soon they have quadruplets. Ernie is ruined.

In the hospital waiting room the new father is besieged by corporate representatives who are anxious to give the parents diapers, food, cribs, prams. Ernie declares himself Gunther's agent.

105. BILKO'S PRIZE POODLE 6/6/58

Bilko has been writing dozens of letters for Doberman to a pen pal named Louise. She informs him that she is being married – to the postman. Duane is devastated. He applies for a transfer to Alaska because he wants to forget. The transfer will take some time. Bilko gives him $5 to go into town see a movie and pig out. Doberman buys a french poodle puppy for only five dollars, because she has no pedigree papers, and names the dog Louise. Surprisingly, pedigree papers do come. Louise is fully grown. Bilko enters her in the annual dog show in New York at just about the time that Doberman is transferred to Alaska. The dog pines for Doberman. Bilko uses flim-flam techniques and gets Doberman back from Alaska just as the judging begins at the dog show. The joyful canine wins 'first in class'. The judge checks the pedigree papers. He disqualifies the poodle because the papers are *for* a Doberman, not *to* Doberman.

106. BILKO'S SCHOOL DAYS 13/6/58

Bilko is elated when 1,500 MPs in training arrive at Fort Baxter. New pigeons, new money. They have been authorised to arrest anyone breaking the smallest regulation. Bilko can't beat them so he becomes an MP trainee. He knows every rule in the book. Soon he is in charge of a platoon of MPs. His aim is to have all the regular personnel put in the guardhouse. Without experienced people, Fort Baxter will come to a standstill. His platoon is arrested – so no motor pool. The mess sergeant is arrested – so no food. Even his girl, Joan Hogan, is

'Bilko's Prize Poodle'

arrested along with all the WACs who perform office duties. The MPs are ordered to move their school to North Dakota. The colonel is delighted – Bilko will have to move with the MPs. Bilko spills ink on the colonel's desk and orders his own MPs to arrest him for defacing government property. He won't have to go to North Dakota.

107. JOAN'S BIG ROMANCE 27/6/58

Joan Hogan is leaving for Chicago on furlough. Bilko is seeing her off – more exactly, brushing her off, because he is in a hurry to take Ritzik's money at poker. Joan is severely annoyed. On the train, Randy Vandermeer, a wealthy playboy, slips into the seat beside Joan to escape a photographer. The photographer manages to snap one picture of Joan and Randy, which appears in the papers. Bilko is furious. Joan is informed that Bilko is in a Chicago flop house, drunk and desperate. Joan is on to the master swindler and goes to see his act. She informs the thespian that Randy has asked her to marry him. Bilko rushes off to Vandermeer's apartment. Vandermeer is preparing a private dinner for a lady. It is not for Joan but Bilko does not believe the philanderer. Joan and Ernie make up, fight again, and leave not talking to each other. Back at Fort Baxter they are still not talking but realise how silly that is and make up again.

Season Four 1958/1959

108. GOLD FEVER 26/9/58

Bilko buys a chest at an army-surplus auction and finds a map for a gold mine in California. Henshaw, Rocco and The Bilkster head for California. They find an old army site: Camp Fremont. A surveyor is marking the area, which is to be torn down the following week. Ernie –

using the usual Bilko cunning – informs the colonel that Fort Baxter is being abandoned by the Pentagon. Colonel Hall volunteers to take over Camp Fremont and move all his troops to the pleasant California climate. The colonel and Bilko's platoon go west as an advance party. Bilko has his platoon digging up the area. Each man finds hunks of rock with shiny metal particles imbedded. They're sure that they've found gold. The colonel brings a large chunk of the rock and explains that it's fool's gold that has no value. Even without the gold, the platoon figures that they've got a good deal: Hollywood to the south, San Francisco to the north and Las Vegas to the east.

Note: Once Bilko gets the Fort Baxter gang of military heroes to Camp Fremont, they never return to Rosedale, Kansas.

109. BILKO'S VAMPIRE 3/10/58
Mess Sergeant Ritzik, Bilko's most lucrative pigeon, leaves the nightly poker sessions early. Detective work reveals that Ritzik is rushing to watch vampire movies. The Gypster convinces Ritzik that he is turning into a vampire. The company cook goes for a blood test. Bilko substitutes a tube of bat blood for Ritzik's sample; the medical officer informs the colonel that one of his men has 100 per cent bat blood. Bilko reads that a Hollywood studio is looking for a new actor to play a vampire. When the colonel tells him that Ritzik's blood is pure bat, Bilko offers to take Ritzik to a Hollywood hospital for verification. Instead, Bilko goes to the studio and using the base hospital's blood report, proves that Ritzik has only bat blood. The executives see tremendous publicity potential and sign Ritzik for a $100,000 a year. Ritzik rejects the offer. He doesn't want to scare kids.

Bilko, greedy but with a conscience, tears up the contract.

110. BILKO'S DELUXE TOURS 10/10/58

Rail transit from Camp Fremont to San Francisco is sporadic. Bilko and his accomplices buy a beat-up school bus, fix it up a little, and offer GIs direct service to the Golden Gate city. The railroad issues a new schedule. Five round trips a day at half the fare that Bilko's clunker charges. To salvage its investment The Bilko Bus Company offers a deluxe tour of California: beautiful scenery; stops at parks, including a visit to the Clark Gable Ranch; a meeting with the great actor; and, as a bonus, a meal at the California Inn. Bilko signs up a busload of tourists, some of whom are fooled by one of Bilko's henchmen impersonating Clark Gable. They never see the handsome star – but they do shake his hand through a hedge. Instead of being the cheap hamburger joint that Bilko envisioned, the California Inn is an elegant establishment. Total bill: $97 [remember this was 1958]. Bilko and company are washed up.

111. BILKO, THE POTATO SACK KING 17/10/58

A former member of Bilko's platoon needs a new sales manager for his burlap potato sack company. He remembers Bilko as the best salesman in the world, a man who sold sun lamps in the tropics. He hires Bilko at $20,000, a year [in 1958] to be his sales manager. After the first week the cancellations start pouring in. Plastic potato sacks have been devised and all the big potato farms are buying them. His employer is stuck with 100,000 yards of burlap. Bilko is 'sacked' but, being Bilko, he has a way out. He finds a way to treat the burlap to make army uniforms. A fashion magazine endorses the new army garb. The wives of generals read

'Bilko's Deluxe Tours'

the magazine and persuade their husbands to adopt the new attire. Soldiers in Vienna in 1890 wore similar costumes. Bilko is close to a major order when the army tests the uniforms under heat, cold and tropical rain. After the rain test, the arms and legs of the uniforms have stretched eight inches. No sale!

112. BILKO VS COVINGTON 24/10/58
Sergeant Covington's dances, raffles and gambling nights are attracting the dollars away from Bilko. Bilko receives a letter from an old buddy stationed in Wakovo, Japan, a place covered with volcanic ash. Bilko tells Paparelli that he is going into the cultured pearl business and that he will be leaving for Wakovo. Covington hears the rumours and gets a transfer to Japan ready – until he finds out that there is no body of water near Wakovo. Covington fakes a broadcast about a new drug made from volcanic ash. Bilko orders 300 tons of ash through his friend in Japan. The two sergeants sign a truce dividing the Camp Fremont swindling rights between them. A Japanese government official comes to Fremont. He offers sergeants with technical skills, jobs in Japan – good pay, quarters in a major hotel and so on. Bilko spurns the offer as a Covington ploy. Covington is amused by the amateurish attempt by Bilko. Sergeant Grover accepts the job and is off to the good Japanese life.

113. BILKO JOINS THE NAVY 31/10/58
Bilko, Zimmerman and Paparelli are in San Diego [home port for much of the Navy] with seven dollars among them. They try to get into a Navy craps game but are denied admittance because they're soldiers. They rent naval uniforms, they're granted entry to the game and Bilko wins $1,800. The shore police raid the place, con-

fiscate the winnings and escort the three to a large aeroplane carrier that is heading for Alaska for six months. The insignia on their rented uniforms indicates that they're stewards and they're told to prepare breakfast. When they ask, 'For how many?' they are told, 'Eighteen hundred'. Bilko tries to persuade the first officer to mutiny because the captain is showing symptoms of being crazy (Bilko has seen Caine Mutiny once too often). The officer makes short work of Bilko's fantasy and the three go to confess to the Captain that they are soldiers. They overhear that the ship is stopping in San Francisco for a 36-hour shore leave. The trio is saved.

114. BILKO'S BIG WOMAN HUNT 7/11/58
Bilko sees a young woman in an elevator in the Mark Hopkins hotel in San Francisco. A bomb goes off in his head. Ernie is in love. He tries to reach her; she slips away. He bribes the elevator operator, grabs passers-by – no one knows her. He goes to the police station. The police artist makes a sketch from Bilko's ardent description. Bilko dressed as a bellboy shows the picture to everyone. A man comes to the desk and shows a photograph of Bilko's love to the desk clerk. He says that he is engaged to the young lady. The clerk identifies her as Miss Hawkins who works in the dance studio. Bilko congratulates the man on his coming marriage. The stranger says there will be no marriage. Bilko tries to get Miss Hawkins to give him a lesson but she has to leave. Bilko leaves. A bomb goes off in Miss Hawkins' head. She's in love. She calls the lobby desk and asks that they hold the soldier who is coming down the elevator. The hotel staff try to grab Bilko. He escapes.

'Bilko Joins the Navy'

115. THE BILKOS AND THE CROSBYS 14/11/58

Pvt Lindsay Crosby has been assigned to the Camp Fremont motor pool. Bilko realises that the recruit is the son of Bing Crosby. Lindsay reports to his three brothers about the fine life he is living under Bilko: his own room and breakfast in bed when he awakens at noon. The brothers reason that Bilko is so nice because he is trying to become the great crooner's manager.

Bilko daydreams what life would have been had he been Bing: at the annual Bing Crosby Golf Tournament, Bing Bilko has his four sons running the parking, food, autographed pictures and used-golf-ball concessions. Lindsay also daydreams: he and his brothers are all named Bilko and all four of them are sergeants under Colonel Hall. Hall complains that he could have been a general if it hadn't been for the brothers. Instead of four stars he got four 'Bilkos'.

The three Crosby sons come to see how their brother is making out at Camp Fremont. They tell Lindsay that a record producer wants to being out an album called *The Five Crosbys* but that their Dad has other commitments. Bilko instantly improvises an arrangement of a song, which the four Crosbys and one Bilko perform. The brothers get a message that Bing can make the recording sessions. Bilko's disappointment is soothed with an invitation to spend the weekend with the Crosbys.

116. BILKO'S ALLERGY 21/11/58

Sergeant Wheeler-Dealer is short of gambling funds and persuades Colonel Hall to lend him his tax refund. Shortly thereafter he becomes allergic to playing cards. He tries everything – including wearing a gas mask when he is near cards – but the violent sneezing persists. The doctor hypnotises Bilko and discovers that Bilko has feelings of guilt toward Colonel Hall for all the tricks he

'Bilko's Allergy'

has played on him. The doctor tells Bilko he will be allergic as long as he has these feelings. Suddenly, Bilko treats his superior officer with respect, does his gardening, and arranges a banquet in honour of the colonel's twenty-five years in the army. The colonel is suspicious and worries that Bilko is trying to get rid of him. When the colonel is escorted into the banquet room by an armed guard, he is sure he is being court-martialled. Much to the colonel's surprise he is being fêted. Bilko's allergy is cured.

117. BILKO AND THE CHAPLAIN 28/11/58

The Pentagon wants a platoon from every base in the San Francisco area to attend a meeting of army brass. The colonel orders that the platoon with the best work record for the week will go, thus making sure that it won't be Bilko's unit. Bilko has spent a weekend with a girl he can't get out his mind. Henshaw convinces him that work will enable him to forget Sherry. To the colonel's chagrin, Bilko's group has the best work record. The chaplain goes along to keep an eye on Bilko. The chaplain has a pet project: a centre for military children. An unscrupulous real estate man has terminated the lease of the centre. The chaplain suggests that Bilko should use his guile to get the lease renewed. Bilko poses as a major general looking to buy land. Bilko cautions the broker that the army will only do business with people who treat servicemen and their families right. The real estate man offers the children's centre a new lease. Bilko and Sherry have another weekend of terminal ecstasy.

118. BILKO PRESENTS THE McGUIRE SISTERS 5/12/58

The great bamboozler is setting up another one of his fraudulent concerts. An agent books three great names for the concert. All three have birth certificates or passports to prove who they are, but not the talent that goes with the monikers. There's Frank Sinatra – short and fat who recites poetry; Kim Novak who plays a musical saw; and the McGuire Sisters who are Hungarian acrobats. With names like these the show is sold out. The real McGuire Sisters get a letter from Duane Doberman who expresses his anticipation at being able to see them at Camp Fremont. The kindhearted girls are so touched that they go to California to do the show. Backstage, the acrobatic McGuires and the singing McGuires get into a fight over who are the real performers. Bilko throws the real McGuires out because they have no ID. Doberman shows Bilko an autographed picture that the genuine articles have sent him. Bilko realises his error and runs after the insulted trio. The girls return to the theatre because of Duane. The talented ladies bring the house down. Bilko is standing at the stage door when Mickey Rooney comes in. Bilko chases him out as another impostor.

119. BILKO'S SECRET MISSION 12/12/58

The sergeants and the motor pool leave for Yucca Flats, forty miles from Las Vegas. Testing will be taking place to see the effect of nuclear bombs on army tanks. A scientist at the facility demonstrates a new machine. Anything, including living flesh, that passes through its field becomes 'attractive' – not just to iron and steel, but to anything that comes close to it. The only substance that will counteract the 'magnetism' is alcohol, applied externally or taken internally. Ritzik delivers some snacks to the scientists. The machine has been left on by accident and the unattractive Ritzik becomes very 'attractive'. All the personnel at Yucca Flats have been confined to the site. Bilko and Ritzik get out and into a

Las Vegas casino. They play roulette. Ritzik points at a number and the ball follows his finger. Ritzik and Bilko are ahead by $78,000. Bilko orders champagne for the crowd. Ritzik takes a sip and his 'magnetism' is gone. They lose everything. And to add insult to poverty, the MPs arrest them for breaking out of camp.

120. BILKO'S GIVEAWAY 19/12/58

As usual, Bilko is broke, this time in Hollywood. He hustles his way on to an afternoon quiz show. He is paired with a boy of ten or eleven. The kid knows his stuff and they win all kinds of merchandise worth about $25,000 on the market. Lots of stuff but no dollars. The barracks is filled with refrigerators, air conditioners, vacuum cleaners and what have you. The IRS is after Bilko. They want tax on all the prizes he has acquired: about six thousand dollars. Bilko figures that his safest bet is to give the stuff away. He starts his own quiz show on a Grove City station. Doberman is the first winner and attracts big mail. After seven straight weeks of winning, Doberman announces that he is retiring from the show and that he will give all the gifts he has received to the community chest in Grove City. He also thanks Bilko for supplying him with all the answers.

121. BILKO AND THE MEDIUM 26/12/58

Bilko needs $500 to open a pool room and bowling alley in Grove City (near Camp Fremont). He has no luck arranging a loan, even when he offers the colonel's jeep as collateral. Ritzik receives a cheque for a $1,000 for a raffle that he has won. Rupert and Emma Ritzik go to medium Madame Zaboda every week and follow her advice about financial matters. Bilko finds out and sets up a counter medium. He engages Madame Flossie, who operates out of an empty house using 'spiritual' tricks

'Bilko and the Medium'

devised by Bilko and his henchmen. Madame Zaboda attends Flossie's séance and exposes her as a fraud. Emma hands Zaboda the thousand dollars to keep for her and to advise her how to invest it. Madame Zoboda attempts to skip town with the money but is stopped by Bilko. In gratitude, Emma lends Bilko five hundred dollars. Bilko returns the money to her – he can't stand being rewarded as a good guy – when he isn't.

122. BILKO'S BOPSTER 2/1/59
'Bopster' was a term applied to swing musicians in the 1950s.

After 22 continuous hours of poker, Bilko needs his sleep. A new recruit, Skinny Sanders, disturbs him and the rest of the platoon with the sound of loud radio, drumming, scat singing and the strange language of the bop musician. After a few days of this, Bilko is about to have Skinny transferred to Alaska when he discovers that the Bopster is a famous musician. He suggests that the army organise a goodwill swing group to tour Europe. Ernie will, of course, be the man in charge. Bilko can't find suitable musicians among the soldiers at Camp Fremont. At a San Francisco Swing club he smooth talks the band to enlist in the army. The word 'army' means nothing to these far-out musicians. But Skinny Sanders means a lot. Bilko is just about to leave for Paris with the 'Khaki Six' when a general arrives. He has ordered himself to go with the band on its goodwill tour. Bilko is left behind to organise a second band for the Pacific area.

123. BILKO'S HOLLYWOOD ROMANCE 9/1/59
Monica Malamar is a big Hollywood star – with remarkably bad press, five marriages, slugging cops, fights with directors. To refurbish her image the studio decides that she have a romance with a nice, clean-cut GI. Bilko gets

chosen for the chore. At first he plays the shy, innocent country boy. Slowly the career trickster starts emerging and he mixes into her business more and more. The studio offers Bilko a contract as an actor. Bilko decides he has to break up with Monica – her fast reputation would be a drag on his acting career. He tells her. She laughs at him. He has been had; it's a trick to get rid of him. Bilko goes on the counteroffensive. Monica and Ernie pretend that they are going to get married. He is foregoing an acting career to be Monica's agent. He hands the studio head a contract that calls for Monica to get $400,000 a picture or they go to another studio. The contract is signed. Ernie has his revenge.

124. BILKO'S GRAND HOTEL 30/1/59

The members of the motor pool have invested all of their meagre resources in a pizza stand. On opening day it burns down because of Paparelli and Zimmerman's carelessness. Bilko sells Ritzik's car to get funds to continue their foray into the hospitality business. They buy a broken-down hotel with a down payment of three hundred dollars. Chester Hilton, a homeless character, is elected president of their new venture, thus giving them the right to name it The Grove City Hilton. The use of that prestigious name is not for attracting customers. Bilko hopes that the Hilton chain will buy the ramshackle building so as not to tarnish their trademark. Very soon, the Hilton people agree to give him $5,000 for his beat-up building. Just as the contract is about to be signed, the Grove City Hilton burns down – Zimmerman and Paparelli at work again.

125. BILKO'S CREDIT CARD 6/2/59

Bilko has been embarrassed on a date when he lacks the cash to cover the bill. He tries to take out a credit card and is vehemently turned down [unlike 2000 when credit cards are forced on every unworthy risk]. The slippery sergeant decides to found the GIs' Gourmet Club. This is one Bilko scheme that sounds dimly legitimate. Soldiers sign for their drinks and meals. When they are paid, they pay Bilko, who deducts a small commission and pays the eating places. Bilko is about to start collecting the money due to him when three battalions at the fort are sent away for a couple of weeks to participate in war games. The restaurateurs threaten Bilko with fists and the DA if he doesn't come up with the money in 24 hours. Typical Bilko charades get the three battalions back to Camp Fremont. Bilko and cronies collect the money due to them and pay off the restaurants.

126. VIVA BILKO 13/2/59

Bilko takes Zimmerman, Rocco and Doberman on a trip to Mexico. At a famous club they are held up by four *banditos*. The soldiers are forced to exchange their uniforms and papers for Mexican garb. The desperadoes, wearing US Army uniforms, rob a bank. The Bilko tour group is now wanted by the Mexican police. Bilko and cohorts try to get back into the States wearing Mexican clothes. They have no ID and the US immigration officials refuse them admittance. Bilko and his desperate friends try being smuggled into their own country, to no avail. In a most complicated plot, they change from Mexican garb to their uniforms and back again several times. Finally the army gets word to the immigration people to allow Bilko and colleagues back into the good old USA. They pass through the barriers and are immediately arrested by MPs. They've been out of the country for seven days on three-day passes.

127. THE COLONEL'S PROMOTION 20/2/59
The colonel is furious. Once again he has been passed over for promotion to brigadier general. The colonel has decided that if he is not given a promotion he will leave the army. Mrs Hall is worried about her husband and talks to the chaplain who talks to Bilko. The colonel leaves for Washington. If Hall leaves the army, the chaplain tells Bilko, a new commander will not be tolerant of Bilko's gambling and regulation flouting. In Washington, Bilko hooks up with the colonel and persuades him that smart is better than tough. A lobbyist is scheduled for a round of golf with the president. Bilko sees to it that the lobbyist is delayed and Hall completes the president's foursome. Word gets around fast in Washington and, even though Duffer Hall barely breaks 150, he has become *persona grata*. The colonel returns home with stars in his eyes but *not* on his shoulders. He has turned down the promotion because it meant leaving Camp Fremont and its hotchpotch of whimsical soldiers.

128. BILKO'S SHARP SHOOTER 27/2/59
Bilko is supervising the targets at rifle practice. One of Ritzik's platoon hits the bull's-eye nine times out of ten. Ritzik is cleaning up betting on him. Another marksman hits the target *ten* times out of *ten*; Bilko tries to track him down. He makes a mistake and thinks that Emil Schneider is the sharpshooter. Bilko sets up a match and Emil hits everything in the vicinity except the target. Bilko finds out that his 'man' is a WAC, Polly Porter from Texas. She has been using the shooting range without permission. Bilko invites her to join his 'gun club'. Polly tells Ernie that she is being transferred to another camp the next day. Bilko cons the colonel into believing that he is about to marry Polly and the colonel changes her orders. Bilko sets up a match between Polly and Ritzik's

champion. The two sharpshooters look at each other, fall in love, and do an Emil Schneider – they hit everything in the vicinity but the target.

129. BILKO'S FORMULA SEVEN 6/3/59
A member of the platoon, about 40, with a wrinkled face, has brought a jug of moonshine into the motor pool. When the colonel unexpectedly arrives, the man gets rid of the hooch by pouring it into the engine of a jeep. The colonel leaves. Bilko orders the mountain man to drain the engine. He gets the motor oil and applejack mixture on his face. After his shower the wrinkles are gone. The colonel is under a hot towel in the barbershop. Bilko puts some of the sludge on the officer's face. The colonel emerges appearing much younger. Bilko is sure that he has discovered an oily fountain of youth. He starts manufacturing Formula Seven in the shop by running the mountain dew through jeep engines. Deborah Darling, the CEO of a major cosmetic company, has the stuff tested and threatens Bilko with prosecution because he has violated Federal Drug Administration regulations.

130. BILKO'S APE MAN 20/3/59
Pvt Forbes; tall, handsome, well muscled, is in Bilko's platoon. He was a physical training instructor in civilian life. The colonel has assigned him to the motor pool so that he can make the group of slovenly soldiers into recognisable human beings. A film studio is looking for a new Tarzan; Forbes is just the man. He is entered in the Mr Universe contest and Bilko goes along with him. In an attempt to ensure Forbes' winning, Bilko tries to induce the editor of a woman's magazine to vote for Forbes. She yells for the police. The pushy sergeant is thrown out and Forbes is disqualified. Bilko needs

'Bilko's Formula Seven'

another gimmick to call attention to his man ... Like fighting a gorilla. Perfectly safe. Doberman plays the gorilla. Through field glasses, the colonel catches sight of Doberman practising his part. To protect the base and the surrounding community the colonel orders out 3,000 riflemen with instructions to shoot the gorilla on sight. Bilko arrives in time to save Doberman for another episode.

Note: Lucille Ball plays a small part in this episode – a somewhat wacky fan of the Mr Universe competition. She is extremely beautiful and very funny. There is no credit for her performance.

131. WARRANT OFFICER PAPARELLI 27/3/59
Bilko and the motor pool gang have been caught by the lieutenant neglecting their work and gambling. Punishment: a long hike with heavy backpacks. Luck is with them: the officer is transferred. Bilko feels that any new officer assigned to them will be equally tough so the schemer decides to make his own officer. Paparelli is chosen. He is docile enough to do Bilko's bidding, no matter what his rank.

General Wheeler is inspecting Camp Fremont. Bilko stages several 'dangerous' incidents and, in each case, Paparelli saves the general's life. The general makes Dino a warrant officer. Paparelli proves to be the kind of obedient superior that Bilko has always wanted. Colonel Hall inspires Paparelli to be a disciplinarian and an honourable officer. Bilko has made Dino an officer and he can unmake him. He sends him an invitation to a costume party given for the general. The only costume Paparelli can find is a pair of Chinese pyjamas. When the general and colonel find him in the colonel's house in pyjamas, Dino is suddenly a private again.

132. BILKO'S GODSON 3/4/59

Bilko's buddy names his son after Ernie and also makes him the child's godfather. Bilko takes the child in his carriage to the park. A young father tells Bilko that he will be registering his son for Yale. Bilko counters that his godson will go to Stanford. The next day he tries to register the baby at Stanford. The school will accept such a reservation only from someone who has been a student at Stanford. Bilko wants to enrol himself at the university but realises that he can never pass the entrance exam. A member of his platoon, a history buff, will take part of the exam; his bookmaker will take the math; an ex-prisoner is a whiz at science, he has studied the subject while behind bars. Bilko has worked out three scams to clear the room before each exam. While the room is clear, Ernie's stand-ins take their part of the exam. The three score high. Ernie, now a Stanford student, is assured his godson's place in the school is safe.

133. GUINEA PIG BILKO 17/4/59

Bilko usually sleeps till 11 a.m. The colonel has the payroll distributed in the early morning. Bilko wakes up early, with a feeling that something is wrong. He rushes to the paymaster's office and finds his platoon getting paid. He stands at the door, furious, and as the platoon passes he snatches money out of their hands. Major Anderson wants to test a drug for 'Hyperactivity Neurosis' – a condition where the patient can't concentrate on military duties and is obsessed with gambling and scamming; a perfect description of Bilko. Anderson gives Bilko a couple of capsules and the lion becomes a lamb. Captain Barker reports that the platoon has become greedier than Bilko at his worst. They're running a wide-open gambling room. Major Armstrong admits that his drug is a failure. It cancels ordinary aggressiveness and leadership. The colonel needs to shock Bilko out of his calm state. He orders fifty-thousand dollars to be brought from the base safe and be placed in front of the gambling meister. The sight of all that money snaps Bilko out of it.

134. BILKO THE BUTLER 24/4/59

Bilko attends a wedding. The groom is a GI; the bride is an heiress. They met at a San Francisco USO. Bilko is jealous. The bride is pretty and her father is very rich. Bilko goes to the USO. The Seeker-After-Married-Wealth has Sunday dinner in a Nob Hill home. His host and hostess are the butler and his wife. A telephone call and the butler must prepare for thirty or forty guests that very evening. Bilko insinuates himself as the second butler. He does more hustling than 'butling'. Over-hearing news of a merger, he phones his buddies to buy stock. He reveals that he has hidden cash in the muzzle of a rifle. A little later he discovers that the rumours of a merger are bogus. Back at Camp Fremont his buddies have been arrested. They had taken the rifle to the tele-graph office to send the money to a broker. The MPs thought that they were holding up the place and confis-cated the rifle. Bilko's money is safe.

135. RITZIK GOES CIVILIAN 1/5/59

Once again, Ernie Bilko has won all of Ritzik's money. Ritzik's wife makes him leave the army just to get away from Sergeant Clip-Artist. Bilko feels bad, but not bad enough to give Rupert back his money. The Ritziks get duped when they buy a diner from the local bank: busi-ness is terrible. Bilko's guilty conscience makes him visit the Ritziks and, seeing the serious trouble they're in, he goes into flimflam mode. The president of the bank is

'Bilko the Butler'

also the mayor of the town. Bilko and his regular accomplices pretend to be army journalists and con the mayor/bank president into giving Ritzik back double the money he paid for the diner. Bilko feels that Ritzik's future belongs in the army where he is close to a pension. Emma won't let him rejoin as long as Bilko is in the same army. Bilko, dressed in loud civilian clothes, convinces Emma and Rupert that he is out of the service. Ritzik returns to Camp Fremont to re-enlist.

136. BILKO'S SMALL CAR 8/5/59

Colonel Hall sends Bilko into Grove City to pick up his new, just arrived, foreign car. Bilko uses the little car to transport illegal gambling equipment. The police discover the illegal cargo and impound the car. Bilko 'confesses' to the colonel that he damaged the bumper of the little beauty. The car will be fixed in a couple of days. A desperate Bilko and the motor pool team put together their own version of a small car using all kinds of used car parts and a jeep motor. The police return the colonel's authentic car, but Bilko's strange little hybrid has caused so much favourable comment, that he and the motor pool decide to produce the 'Arrivederci' in small quantities. The scrap parts are easily come by but the jeep engines are another thing. Using several ingenious swindles Bilko convinces the colonel to condemn ten jeeps so that he can get his ungreasy hands on the motors. The colonel catches on, orders the ten jeeps restored and Bilko is marched off to the guardhouse.

137. DOBERMAN: MISSING HEIR 15/5/59

Bilko sees Lord and Lady Montague on TV asking for information about a son they haven't seen for 35 years. Their child had a birthmark on his left arm. Bilko believes there is a resemblance between Lady Montague and Doberman. Duane has a birthmark on his left arm. Doberman is accepted as the missing son and is tutored in the speech, manners and *snobbishness* of his new station. He cuts Bilko off. Bilko is miffed because he has lost his chance to be the business manager of a man who will have $50 million. To retain his hold over the heir, Bilko lets loose stripper Dixie on Doberman. Duane asks Bilko to be best man at his wedding to Dixie. The Montague's real son has been found. Birthmark and blood tests check out. Doberman is happy to be a GI again but a poor soldier is the last thing Dixie wants.

138. BILKO'S CASINO 22/5/59
For an infraction, the colonel 'volunteers' the services of Bilko and his troops to clean up a USO Centre in an old house in Grove City. It turns out that this house sits on the only land in California where gambling is legal. A local law passed in the 1860s exempted this acreage from gaming restrictions. The Bilko gang touts service people *away* from the USO. The USO gives up its lease, which is snapped up by Bilko. Opening night is set for The Hacienda Club. Bilko is approached by the elegant but menacing chief of the local mob. He is forced to give the mob all of the income the Hacienda will make. Bilko sends an anonymous letter to the chief mobster warning him that the FBI may be on his tail. The mob lawyer thinks the entire story that gambling was legal in that particular spot may be a sting. The mob wants out and signs the lease over to the USO. The platoon refurbishes the place to USO standards. For once, they're involved in a legitimate enterprise.

139. THE COLONEL'S SECOND HONEYMOON 29/5/59

The heat at Camp Fremont is unbearable. Bilko asks for furlough. Colonel Hall turns him down. The Scheming Sergeant wants to get the colonel out of camp because, when Captain Barker is in charge, Ernie can always get his way. General Wade, a good friend of the colonel, comes for a visit. Mrs Hall and the general have been friends for many years. General Wade gently flirts with Nell and the colonel is irate. Bilko does his wicked best to exacerbate the quarrel. Bilko encourages the colonel to take his wife on a second honeymoon. They head for the 'coolth' of Sun Valley. Captain Barker gives the manipulator furlough and he also heads for Sun Valley. To help the colonel feel that he is an attractive man, Bilko spreads the word that John Hall is a famous movie producer in search of talent. The term 'movie producer' brings out the best – or the worst – in the girls of Sun Valley and they pursue him. The colonel realises that the only woman he wants is Nell. Score one for Bilko: a marriage is saved.

140. BILKO IN OUTER SPACE 5/6/59

Sergeants Ritzik and Grover win $600 in a craps game. They are going to use the money to go to Hawaii in three days. In the fear that Bilko will hear of their winnings and will 'poker' it away from them, they hide in the kitchen freezer, stay out all night sleeping in a car and a pup tent. Bilko is frantic. Six hundred dollars waiting to be won. They elude him. Zimmerman and Paparelli convince Ritzik and Grover that volunteers to stay in a mock-up of a space capsule are needed. They will be in 'space' for three days. What better way to elude Ernie? Just as Sergeant Space-Hoax is about to enter the capsule, Colonel Hall orders Bilko to drive him to an army conference. When Bilko gets back, three days later,

'Bilko in Outer Space'

there is just one hour left to the experiment. He goes into the capsule and the money changes hands. Colonel Hall makes Bilko return the money to Ritzik and Grover. They start their furlough. Bilko, Henshaw and Rocco enter a capsule of their own – the guard house.

141. THE BILKO BOYCOTT 12/6/59

Bilko has surpassed even his own greed. The men turn on him. His sidekick, Henshaw, ashamed of all the money they have drained from the platoon, forms a Gambler's Anonymous unit. Bilko is desperate for pigeons. There are two thousand WACs on post – drawing their monthly pay. In the name of gender equality Bilko decides that they should lose their money just like the men. He initiates a series of lectures that are really gambling games in code. The democratic trickster is going to San Francisco and needs weekend money. He sneaks into the WACs' barracks to collect the loot owed to him. A nurse quarantines the barracks – measles has been reported among the women soldiers. Bilko needs a dime to call for help. One WAC gives it to him – for twenty-five dollars. On the phone Bilko promises Henshaw that he will behave if his former accomplice will rescue him. Bilko gets to sleep in his own bed. He wakes up the next morning with measles.

142. WEEKEND COLONEL 19/6/59

Camp Fremont. A TV camera is mounted in the experimental lab; the colonel has a monitor on his desk. The first experiment he sees is Bilko and the soldiers in a crap game: Ernie caught red-handed. Every building in the base is wired up. Bilko is looking for a way to out-manoeuvre the TV eye. The colonel is away. In a diner Bilko notices the short-order cook is a dead ringer for the colonel. Bilko hires him to impersonate the colonel. The

'The Bilko Boycott'

'colonel' orders the TV monitor to be taken out and permits Bilko to put on a Monte Carlo Night in the officers' club. The real colonel returns home early. He stops in the diner for a cup of coffee and is mistaken for the short-order cook. When the colonel gets back to the base, odd remarks from people who assume that he has been in camp all day, arouse his suspicions. He returns to the diner and gets the story from the cook. Next day the colonel is watching his closed-circuit TV: his favourite show – the guard house with Bilko, Henshaw and Rocco behind bars.

And thus endeth one of the best comedy series ever seen on Television.

THE PHIL SILVERS PONTIAC SPECIAL

KEEP IN STEP 23/1/59
A one-hour broadcast, sponsored by Pontiac.
Written by Billy Friedberg, Arnie Posen, Coleman Jacoby, Terry Ryan
Directed by Aaron Ruben, Al DeCaprio
Guests: Sid Chaplin, Diana Dors and the Bilko Platoon.

This show, which was well reviewed, featured the standard Bilko plot plus songs and choreography. It was an early tape show, filmed before a 'live audience'. Edward Montagne, producer of the show, recollects that at that time, videotape editing was primitive and time consuming. The show was to be aired the day after taping, so the crew had to stay up all night to get it done. Montagne says that Phil Silvers could not pronounce the sponsors' name Pontiac – it came out 'Potniac'. But whether you call it a Pontiac or a Potniac, with Phil Silvers driving, it had to be a very witty car.

'Keep in Step'

Afterword

These days, when clocks run much faster, artifacts a mere 45 years old are ancient, clothes from the 1950s are quaint, kitchen appliances – primitive, cars – fossils, bikinis not cut to the top of the thigh – prudish, black and white TV sets – prehistoric. Programs shown on those sets – corny.

We won't flog it – you get the point.

Phil Silver's Bilko in the year 2000 is as inventive, duplicitous and as original as he was in 1955.

In order to write the summaries of the shows in the Bilko series we had to screen videotape recordings of all the episodes in a four- or five-week period. You'd think looking at 70 hours of a single old series would be a bore and a chore. We did, too.

We were wrong!

Phil Silver's Bilko in a new century is as inventive, wicked and as much fun as he was in 1955. The dialog still bristles with originality, pertinent asides and craftiness as when the sound track was originally laid down. No wonder there are people who have watched these satires of life in the American army thirty or more times. Almost fifty years after their creation viewers still find fresh nuggets of humor at every showing.

Most program descriptions found in magazines or on the Internet are undernourished little sentences, totaling perhaps twenty words. And telling you little about the program.

We wanted our summaries to be something more, to give the reader a true idea of what the show was all about. So each one is at least 150 words. But even with the luxury of so many words, the Bilko plots are complicated and very often have several sub-themes. So, we had to stick to the basic premise of each show and trim words and sentences to essentials of the story line. A complete appreciation of the subtleties of the episodes can be derived only by viewing the tapes. Watching these tiny movies, one becomes aware that the writers of the scripts understood what drove American life in that era. Fifty years later the technology of living in the United States has changed a great deal – but the people of America have not changed so very much.

Phil Silvers' mastery of the thespian trade is remarkable. He schemes wickedness but radiates goodness. He is a lovable scamp. His mobile face underscores his dialogue and his body language is as loud as his spoken words.

His acting abilities have rubbed off on his colleagues and the series is ensemble acting at its best.

Surprisingly, watching the complete series, we discovered that Bilko could not have made a living as a con man or poker player. He loses much more often than he wins.

He really needs his army pay to get along.

And when he does win he is so compassionate that he gives the sucker back his cash.

Recently, the AP reported that Kris Tait, a 25-year-old British woman, was in Tibet wearing a T-shirt imprinted with a likeness of Phil Silvers as Sergeant Bilko. A crowd gathered; people angrily pointed to the shirt and yelled: 'Dalai Lama, Dalai Lama'. A Chinese soldier tried to tear the shirt off her body but she crossed her arms and was able to escape. Silvers was bald and wore glasses. The exiled god-king, has his head shaven and also wears glasses. The AP piece said that Bilko is a British cult figure because of repeated reruns of the show.

Phil Silvers, of course, was not a great religious leader nor a world respected philosopher. Certainly no one's god king. But he does have fans who hold him in great esteem half a century later – a cult of followers who have to have a 'fix' of Bilko every so often – to counteract the hectic pace and laugh-starved days of the 21st century.

MF
SR